Life's Journey

In the Valley

Qiana Tucker

Author

Enhanced DNA
DEVELOP. NURTURE. ACHIEVE.
Publishing Division

Life's Journey
In the Valley
Copyright © 2021 Qiana Tucker
All rights reserved.

ISBN-13: 978-1-7351349-8-7
Library of Congress Control Number: 2020925947

Visit us at
www.historypress.com

Dedication

I would like to dedicate this book to:

My Husband, you have been there through it all. You believed in me when I struggled to see it for myself and encouraged me to keep allowing the Lord to use me despite how I felt or what it looked like. I want you to know that I see the sacrifices you make, and I love and appreciate you more than you may know.

My Children, you all have been the reason behind my why. I am still learning how to be the best mom to you that I can be. Remember how I raised you and never give up on yourself. Always trust in the Lord and know that he will never leave your side. I love you all so much.

My Mom, you have been my solid since day one. You have supported me when no one else would and even when things flopped, you remained. Being a teen mom was not easy, but you made it easier for me just by being there. I appreciate you for all you have done and still do for us. You showed me the true strength of a woman and I love you.

My Pops, thank you for always being there for me. You took me in as your own and never showed any difference. Thank you for always listening and giving wise advice. I love you.

My Sisters, because I am the oldest, I knew that I had to stand strong to be a good example for you all. We have a bond that no one can break. I love you all.

My True Friends, thank you for the tuff love, long suffering, prayers and words of encouragement. You all showed me what the love of Christ looks like in human form. I love you all.

Acknowledgements

All praise and glory to God for what He has made possible for me, if not for Him I would not be here today. I want to thank my family and friends who have been on this journey with me, praying for me, challenging me and laboring with me. I love and appreciate all of you.

Qiana Tucker

Table of Contents

Is it a Good Fight?

I was reading an article about how Christians are to approach someone who has backslid. It spoke about how we are not to come with an iron fist, straight condemning them. On the contrary, they should come with a spirit of humility, gentleness and love. Every time we have a disagreement with someone, that does not mean that we need to prove our point. It may be a time to remain silent and just pray. The flesh side in most of us, wants to vindicate ourselves and get the last word. We feel like if we can get our point across, then we've won the fight or at the least make them see from our view. That is not always the case, we could possibly do more harm than good. The words you speak have a lasting effect on people. Our words can cut deep leading to affliction, or bring comfort, healing and restoration. We must be careful to think about what we say and how it will impact those who hear. There will be a time to speak and a time to be silent. We must pray for maturity in this area, so that we can know the difference. Ask yourself beforehand, is this a good fight?

Read Proverbs 16:24; Galatians 6:1-2 ; Ephesians 4:29

Don't Hold Yourself Hostage to Your Mistakes

I recently done something that I was not proud of. In my mind, I was rationalizing how it wasn't all wrong. But, in my heart, I knew that it wasn't all good either. I felt an overwhelming spirit of conviction. I was sulking all day, even after I repented. We can trick ourselves into believing that our actions are justified, but in the eyes of the Lord, they're wrong. If you have the slightest feeling that somethings not right, do not do it! It wasn't until I read a verse of scripture about forgiveness, that I felt free and forgiven. I felt the peace of God and I heard, God is faithful, even when we're not. We will not be perfect or sinless while we're in these bodies. Now, this in no way excuses our bad behavior. It assures us that if we go to God with a heart of sincerity, repentance and thanksgiving, then He will forgive us. If He forgives us, then we need to forgive ourselves. Don't be so hard on yourself when you fall short. Get up, repent and don't do it again. Stop condemning yourself, you are free and forgiven!

Read Romans 3:22-24, 7:18-25, 8:1-2; 2 Corinthians 7:10; 2 Timothy 2:13 (NLT); 2 Peter 3:9; 1 John 1:9

Take Another Look

Many of us can attest to the fact that we've grown inpatient while waiting on God to move. I was reading the story about when Elijah prayed for rain. God had already told him that He was going to send the rain, so why did he pray for it? Elijah had just been given the victory over all the false prophets of Baal. Such a victorious feat could have easily caused him to fall into pride and caused the people to err as well. God wants us to constantly admit our dependence on Him. Some things will just come, while some will require more prayer and time spent with God. Just because you don't see it yet, doesn't mean it's not coming. We must learn to be patient, live dependent on God and have faith. Keep on looking until you see the manifestation of that which God has spoken.

Father I pray that every vision and everything you've spoken will come to fruition. Readjust our focus and bless us to see by faith. Give us the courage to look again, and again, until you bring to pass what you've spoken. Help us to depend on you and walk by faith, not sight. Thank you for hearing and answering our prayers. In Jesus name amen.

Read 1 Kings 18:1-2, 41-46

The High Maintenance Christian

As I sit and ponder on the condition of the church, it raises questions in my mind. During my journey as a believer, I have experienced many highs and lows. I have yet to meet the perfect, sinless person. I have yet to meet a pastor or leader who has it all together. Yet, some people seem to think they are to be esteemed more than others. This thought and action has led a lot of believers into the spirit of pride and idolatry. We can't go around feeling like we're entitled to certain privileges and treatment. In all instances Jesus himself pushed aside being glorified. He didn't want gifts or have specific demands or requests for things. He even sent out his disciples with just the clothes on their backs, no food and no money. I'm not saying that it's wrong to want or have nice things. But when we feel like we're entitled, and people don't meet our demands, we must check ourselves. Why do you need it? What's the reason for the treatment you're desiring to receive? Our Lord and Savior was beaten, unaccepted in society, mocked and ultimately killed. Yet he didn't ask for anything or complain about it. Some of his followers even suffered in the same manner. So, be careful not to become a high maintenance believer. Follow the example that Jesus spoke of in the Bible, not the one the that's been put out before us. Love and God bless.

Read Isaiah 53:2-3; Luke 9:1-6; Philippians 2:5-8

Come As You Are

I was talking to my sister in Christ, and we were talking about proper attire to wear to church. We talked about how some have taken the "come as you are" cliché, as approval of wearing whatever they want, with no standards. As we continued our discussion, I got a download in my spirit. While our clothes won't keep us out of heaven, our hearts will. God wants us to come to Him as we are which means, broken, tired, sorry for doing wrong, struggling, humble, not all together, etc. When we come to Him honest like this, He receives us. The change happens from the inside out. We will begin to walk in progressive sanctification. What this means is as each day passes, we should be doing better than the last and sinning less and less. Don't get discouraged if you aren't seeing as much spiritual growth as you'd like. Just know that when you come, God is going to move on your behalf. I want to challenge those of you waiting to 'get right', to come to Jesus just as you are. Then, watch, wait and keep the faith.

I hear the Lord saying,

"I will not push you away come, come to me as you are. I love you and nothing can ever separate you from my love children. You are blessed when you're broken because that's where you'll find me. Come to me now. Don't wait another day, come my child come. I will not push you away. I love you more than you can comprehend. Come to me. Come to me. Come to me!"

Read Matthew 11:28; Hebrews 10:22

Fear vs Faith

God made the world by speaking a word. What we see was created by the One we can't see, but what we see is real. The things I tend to fear, are things that can be seen or felt. As believers, we are to move by faith and not lean to our understanding of things. This walk requires for us to see and believe that the things we don't see are real and the things we hope for will come to pass. It's a constant tug of war, but with the help of God, our faith will trump our fears. As I pondered on these thoughts, I got this acronym for,

FEAR

Fighting the feeling of how I'll

Exist in a place that's unknown and

Absolutely makes no natural sense to go to but I am totally

Relying on God to see me through.

So, my fears lead me right into the arms of God by faith.

Read Proverbs 3:5-6; Hebrews 11:1-13

The Great Abandonment

I grew up in a single parent household. My mom did an amazing job raising my sisters and me. However, the absence of proper love and affection from my father, caused a great void and hurt in my life. It left me feeling unloved and abandoned and the feelings grew as I got older. These feelings often led me to make poor choices, which intensified the pain and feeling of rejection. When I came to the knowledge of the Lord, I realized that He was the missing piece I had been looking for. He opened my eyes to see that I was not alone. In the good, bad and sad times He's there. I had to abandon my ways and cling to His ways and love. Be encouraged in the fact that you're never alone. God is right there every step of the way.

Read Psalm 27:10; Matthew 28:20

Try Again

We're often tempted to give up after a failed attempt. A failed attempt doesn't always mean that it's not meant to be. God is teaching us in those moments how to be persistent and never give up. He's also teaching us that he moves on his time frame, not ours. In my failed attempts, I've learned what not to do and how to go about doing it the next time. You grow in those moments, so you can't see it as wasted time. God can use your worse turnout to set you up for your greatest comeback. I encourage you to revisit those areas where you've failed. Pray, use discernment and move with caution. Go where God is leading you and don't doubt that it's him. Complete the work He assigned to you. It's time to try again.

Read Judges 20:17-48; Luke 5:4-6

What About Me?

This seems to be the question on a lot of our minds. What about me? So many of us have gotten discouraged while waiting on the promises of God. You look around and see other people getting healed, being delivered and receiving breakthrough in areas of their lives. You try not to hate on them and grow bitter, but you can't help asking, Lord, when will it be my turn? We can't allow ourselves to get stuck in that thought. You really don't know what all they had to go through to get there. It may just be their season to shine in that way. God has not forgotten about you. I know this seems to be a repetitive saying, but it's so true. You must see things from another perspective and realize just how much you're already blessed. Learn to celebrate with others when they get blessed. Don't hate or be envious but instead, rejoice with them that rejoice! God will take care of you and do just what He said. Your responsibility is to have faith, be obedient and wait. This is not an easy task, but it is possible with God's help. Some of us have tried everything but Him. God is knocking at the door of your heart and asking you the same question, what about me? Will you give Him a try? Be encouraged in the Lord!

Read Luke 15:25-32; Romans 12:15; Revelation 3:20

Wait, Don't Faint!

We are faced with so much from day to day, minute to minute. We encounter things that are inevitable, beyond our control and things that happen as a result of bad decisions. I am pressed to tell you to not faint, but to keep waiting on the Lord. You may have been waiting for days, months or years, just don't give up. There's a lot to learn in the waiting room. God uses everything to our advantage and for His glory. You may not see that in the situation you're going through, but He is. I pray that you all will see from another perspective. I pray your eyes will open and see God working in your favor. He promised to deliver if we ask. He may not reveal how he's going to do it or how long it will take but know that He is. So, wait and don't faint.

Read Psalm 27:13-14; Isaiah 40:31; Matthew 7:7-8; Galatians 6:9

From Begging And Borrowing To Lending, Giving And Trusting

I am steady learning how to trust God. At almost every turn, it seems like my commitment and trust in Him is challenged. You see, one week I'll be high and confident and the next, I'm trying to figure out how things are going to come together. This is not the way it's supposed to be. We can't trust God one week and then start questioning if He is going to do it. We must learn how to trust Him when we see no way out. We must praise Him regardless of what it looks like. God desires for us to prosper. He doesn't want us depending on anyone or anything but Him. Even after begging and borrowing, we can still come up short, so why do it. His Word says, the righteous are never forsaken nor do we beg for bread. So, where did this beggar mentality come from? How did the fear of lack creep in? If God made a way before, he will surely do it again. He is not short of anything. We must learn to trust God with all that we have and know that he will provide.

Read Deuteronomy 15:6; Psalm 37:25; Isaiah 55:10-11; Matthew 4:4; Romans 10:17

The Shaking Is For Your Breaking And Making

God has allowed a great disturbance to occur in some of our lives. We think that it's bad, but, it's all good. The shaking isn't sent to kill or destroy you. It happened to break you down just enough for you to see your need for God. You will not die, and God is still there. We all have a free will, so instead of forcing our will, God allows things to happen to get our attention and humble us. Your broken condition isn't your final state. God is going to use it to rebuild you and make you better. So, don't get frustrated and discouraged during the process. Let God shake up, break up and make you as He desires. You won't regret it. You will see very soon just what it was for.

Read Hosea 2

Love Lifted Me

As I sit and think about the many times, I've felt rejected, abandoned and unloved, I can't help but wonder how I made it through. I thought that no one cared. I thought that no one was there to pick up the broken pieces of my heart. I was unaware of God's love for me. I didn't realize at the time that God was there, and he was lifting me up and out of my troubles. It was His love that didn't allow me to stay drowning in my sorrow and pity. It was His love that didn't allow me to end it all, when I felt like there was no reason for me to live anymore. You see, God's love reaches us wherever we are in life. His love goes deeper than an oceans depth. It stretches farther than the east is from the west. It's unending. It's incomprehensible. It's His love....oh my God your love.

Read Psalm 34:18-19, 40:2-3, 103:9-14, 136:1

It's All About Jesus

My life is far from perfect and I have learned that I don't have to look like or express in my actions, what I am going through. I used to get so down and discouraged when I got hit with challenging times. But God has shown me that even in those moments, He can still use me. People are watching us, and we may be the only light that some will see. What you are going through is happening not only to perfect you, but so that others can see how merciful and faithful God is. You don't have time to get stuck in a pity party. God can and will use what you're going through to build you and help others to come out. Don't wait to let God use you, let him use you right where you're at. To God be the glory in all that we endure.

Read Job 13:15; Romans 8:28; Philippians 1:12-19, 4:11-13; 1 Thessalonians 5:18; James 1:2-4

Don't Question, Just Believe

With so many different things to believe in and countless religions to choose from, I choose to believe in The Lord Jesus Christ. I believe that He, God the Father and Holy Spirit are one. I believe that Jesus died for my sins and rose on the third day with all power. I believe that Holy Spirit lives down on the inside of me, empowering me to live right. I believe that He is coming back for His church. I believe there is life after death. I believe that all who trust in Jesus, will live in heaven with him forever. People are going to try to discredit and do everything they can to confuse the truth. Now, I can't tell you how all of this adds up. I just choose not to question it and have faith that it is true. We will not be able to comprehend it all, but you can rest assured that all He says in his Word is true. Just believe, simply just believe.

Read Numbers 23:19; 2 Timothy 2:15-26, 3:13-17

Faith Walkers

It is not easy to see through the eyes of faith when you have trouble on almost every side. In moments like these you need to press harder and keep your faith in God. You must trust Him even when you don't know what's on the other side. We are faith walkers.

Read Luke 1:37; 2 Corinthians 5:7; Hebrews 11:6

Just One Drop

As I was getting out of my car, I looked over and saw a drop of juice on my book. Then I heard the Lord say, just one drop. Have you ever sat and thought about what Jesus did for you when He died on the cross? He gave his life so that we can live and be free. He died for us to have access back to the Father and live forever with him in heaven. No matter how far you go or how much you do, never forget the blood. One drop of His blood cleanses. One drop of His blood heals. One drop of His blood saves. One drop of His blood forgives. One drop of His blood restores. Oh, the blood of Jesus, it will never lose its power!

Read Isaiah 53; Ephesians 1:7; 1 Peter 3:18

Are You Ready For The Rejection

A s I sit and think about some of the things that I've been blessed to have, some of them didn't come on the first try. When I was buying my first house, I experienced quite a few noes before my yes. What I had to understand is that some levels of promotion come with rejection attached. You may have to hear a no before you walk into your yes. The challenge comes when you know that you heard God tell you it's your time, and you move only to get rejected. This is a test of your faith and patience. Are you willing to keep trusting in Him and wait for what he said you can have? You may have to do a little work, but it's worth it in the end. The children of Israel knew what was promised to them. But, somewhere along the way they felt rejected and abandoned by God. I want to encourage you to not give up. Just because your first few times didn't bring the results that you were expecting, doesn't mean it wasn't God. Be prayerful and ask for the Lord to make you more sensitive to hear his voice. So, when you get a no, you won't get discouraged and give up. If it's your time for it, it's coming. Keep your faith in God. Be patient. Be still. Be ready.

Read Psalm 27:13-14; Proverbs 3:5-6; Habakkuk 2:3

Wait And Wait Some More

Why is it that we seem to have less patience with God than we do with people? I am reminded of times in my life when I waited on people to change and they didn't. I spent years of my life waiting, so I could decide on what to do next. I sacrificed a lot with little in return. But, when it came down to me waiting on God to move, I grew impatient. I gave up at times and often felt like it was all for nothing. I had these feelings because I couldn't see in the natural all the benefits from trusting God. I would pray and expect instant results. God doesn't always move like that, sometimes we will just have to wait. It took some things days, some months and some years to manifest. I want to encourage not to give up on waiting for God to do it. Keep trusting and keep believing. He must honor his word. So, wait and wait some more.

Read Psalm 40:1, 130:5-6

The Cover-Up

I was reading the story about David and Bathsheba's adulterous affair. After David slept with her, she became pregnant. He tried everything he could to cover it up. He went as far as having her husband set up to be killed in battle. Ultimately God punished David for his actions.

Some of us have messed up so bad, to where we've covered it up and kept going. Truth is God sees everything that we are doing, and eventually our secrets will come out. You may not get it right now, but there's a day of judgment coming. It's time to get your life in order. Stop trying to cover up your sin and act as if everything is good. Come out, confess and be healed.

Read 2 Samuel 11-12; 2 Corinthians 7:9-10; James 5:16; Revelation 3:3

Why Wait?

My mind takes me back to a time when I put off surrendering my life to the Lord. He would send people to tell me about the gospel, but I wasn't feeling it. I would make slick remarks and get irritated. I used to think that I had all the time in the world to get right. I felt like I had to get it all out of my system before I said yes. I lived a carefree life because I was young and didn't think about dying. I didn't think about the consequences of my actions. God is merciful, but there will come a time when we'll have to leave this place. We will have to answer for what we do and how we live here determines where we'll go. What better time to give your life to the Lord than now? A lady once testified that a family member was asked when he was going to come to the Lord and he replied, I'll do it next week. Guess what, he died less than a week later. Stop pushing God away and putting off making the right decisions. When you feel the urge or hear the call, answer with haste. Tomorrow isn't promised so why wait?

Read Psalm 39:4-5; Proverbs 27:1; Acts 24:24-25; Hebrews 9:27-28

Prepare As You Pray

We sometimes ask for God to do something and we haven't prepared for Him to do it. Don't just pray and wait, pray and prepare. Some of our answers will come with casualties. That means something may die in the process. This death pertains to our sinful desires and hang ups like; lust, greed, ungodly relationships, fornication, fear, lack of faith, drug addiction, alcoholism, hate, pride, holding grudges and whatever else is hard to let go of and shake yourself lose from. God is calling for a death of it. Now, we may not know everything that we need let go of, so I encourage you to check what you're doing against the Word and if it's contrary to it, let it go. Pray and ask for the convicting power of Holy Spirit to pierce your heart. God wants us to experience greater, but first some things need to fall off. Prepare yourself to be free.

Read Matthew 19:16-22, 20:20-23, 26:36-46

God Did It, Not The Devil

Over the course of my life, I've experienced all sorts of heartache and let downs. I used to be quick to say, oh that's the devil messing with me. A lot of us tend to think this when things are torn away from us, or we're denied something. Sometimes this is true and sometimes not. Occasionally, God will allow a great shaking to occur in our lives. He allows it when we're involved with people or activities that we shouldn't be. He may allow an illness, so that he can work a miracle. He allows some things to happen because of our sins. In some cases, He allows doors to close or not open because he knows what is best for us. Whatever state you find yourself in, ask God to give you discernment, because not everything that happens is the enemy messing with you. Ask for Him to reveal His will as you pray through what you endure. God may very well be shaking up some things to humble you and cause you to come back to Him. God wants a yes out of you.

Read Jeremiah 5:10-11; Jonah 1:15-17; Acts 9:1-9; 2 Corinthians 12:6-10

Be Consistent Even When All Else Seems To Fail.

There's so much that takes place in a day. Things will happen that we can't help, so we must learn how to take it all in strides. Keep moving and don't stop doing what you're called and assigned to do. If you fall, don't beat yourself up about it. Get up, keep moving and don't look back. Look to the Lord for strength and guidance to get you through all you endure in your life.

C - Continue with the flow.

O - Operate when opposed.

N - Never give up.

S - Stop doubting.

I - Idleness isn't an option.

S - Stay focused.

T - Trust God.

E - Endure trying times.

N - No looking back.

T – Take nothing for granted.

Who Me?

Why is it that we have such a difficult time believing that God can use us? I'm reminded of something that happened, not long after I got serious about my walk with the Lord. I was unwed and pregnant with my fourth baby. My former pastor, another minister and I went to visit a lady who had just had a terrible car accident. As I sat and listened to them talking, I was like, why am I even here. As we were leaving out, I heard a voice say, tell her not to blame herself. Initially I thought that I was tripping, so I kept walking out. Then, I heard it again. I was like no, I don't know this woman and I'm not telling her that. I kept walking but something in me wouldn't let me leave and kept pressing me to tell her. I finally caved and as soon as I told her, she burst into tears. She said that she hadn't told anyone, but she had been blaming herself for what had happened. I was in complete shock. My pastor came back to see what was going on and I told her what had happened. She told me that I had heard the voice of the Lord. I was like wow, God just used me. This was during a time in my life when I felt useless, unloved and beyond forgiving. At that moment, I believe that God was letting me know that He still loved me and had use for me. All I'm trying to say is, no matter how much you've messed up in life, God is calling your name and has use for you. So, the answer to today's question is, yes you! Now get up and go.

Read Exodus 4:1, 10-13; Jeremiah 1:6-8

Be Faithful And Fruitful During Times Of Affliction

The first thing that some of us tend to do when we face difficulties is push back and retreat. However, not every challenge requires for us to do that. A grape must be pressed and crushed for us to enjoy its juice and an orange goes through a similar process. Our difficult times present the opportunity for us to be a more effective witness for Christ. Although we're being pressed and sometimes crushed, our fruit will be sweet and satisfying. If people see that we're still pushing forward and keeping our faith during challenging times, then our chances of winning them to Christ is increased. So, don't isolate yourself just because you're enduring. It is just one of the many things you'll go through that will lead you up to your greater.

Read Jeremiah 20:7-9; Acts 16:25-34; Timothy 4:1-5

Borrowed Time, Borrowed Things and Borrowed Life

We sometimes make the mistake of thinking that we own things. When, God is only giving us the responsibility of managing what He allows us to have. So, when things go haywire in our lives, we can call on Him to fix it. If we own them, then we rely solely on ourselves to get things done, and this is not what God wants. We are to trust in Him for all things pertaining to life because we can't do it without Him. None of this stuff belongs to us, we are simply borrowing all that's here. We must learn to manage well what God puts into our hands to do and take care of. Give back to God what's His; your life, children, home, job, material possessions etc. Let go of your owner mentality and live your life depending on God.

Read Psalm 24:1; 1 Corinthians 6:19-20

Follow God

We will face making some type of decision daily and what we choose determines what will happen next. Some decisions we make, we choose for the sake of others. While at other times, we do what we feel would benefit us. I have learned that the best move we can ever make is one that God leads us to do. With every move there is a lesson learned, even when it's a wrong move. We can't stop what God does, but we can hinder or slow up where we're going. Be prayerful when you make decisions because what you do can affect others. Follow God, even when it makes no sense to go or to stay.

Read Psalm 37:23-24; Proverbs 14:12; Matthew 4:18-20, 10:38-39

Broken To Live, Not Broken To Die

God will not always reveal why He allows certain things to happen in our lives; if He did, would it make it better or would we still feel the same? In the end, we just   need to let what He allows run its course. I'm reminded of a virus infection, you can take medicine for it, but it still must run its course. We can't take short cuts and shorten the cycle of some of life's events. God is perfecting certain areas of our lives through these things. Some things you can help and some you can't. Rest assured that He will not allow more than you can handle, so let it be and trust him.

Read 1 Corinthians 10:13; 2 Corinthians 4:8-11; James 1:2-4

Too Overwhelmed To Recognize That Jesus Is Right There

I was reading the story of Jesus's resurrection and His appearance to Mary Magdalene. Mary was crying at the gravesite where Jesus was buried, when two angels appeared. The angels asked her why she was crying. As she was replying, she turned around and saw Jesus standing there, but was so overcome with grief, she didn't recognize Him. Some of us are experiencing issues so intense, we can no longer see Jesus is with us. We claim to know Him but have failed to recognize His presence in our lives. Our tears have drowned out our vision and we've forgotten His Word. I encourage you to remember what His Word says and speak it. Don't allow your issues to keep you in a place of deception, believing that Jesus isn't there with you. You are the only one surprised by what happened because he knew about it before it took place. Hold fast to your faith and trust God is with you. No matter what happens in your life, He's always right there. Now, open your eyes. Can you see Him?

Read John 20:11-16

Finding Comfort In The Confusion Of Construction

God has been reconstructing my life over the past year or so. At the beginning of 2017, I heard Him say that it would be a year of turn around and great shifting, little did I know the things that I would face. I cried a lot and I experienced moments of frustration and confusion. I didn't understand why I was enduring some of the challenges that came my way. There were times when I wanted to give up and walk away, but God wouldn't let me. I felt a strength rise in me to keep moving despite my feelings. All my ups and downs were just part of the reconstructing process and God blessed me to find comfort in Him right in the middle of it. As I reflect on the things that I lost and had to let go of, I see it was really setting me up for a greater gain. He's constantly showing me just how much He loves me and wants me. Please understand that He loves you and has your best interest in mind too. Keep moving during the confusion and reconstructing seasons of your life. Don't give up, God will comfort you and see you through. He's waiting for you to surrender.

Read Jeremiah 29:10-14

Use The People On Your Team

I envisioned the people in the body of Christ playing a basketball game. We were on the offense and the enemy was on the defense. When we're dribbling the ball of life and running towards our purpose, we must learn when to pass the ball for help. This isn't a one man show, God didn't put us here to fight alone. He gave us each other to assist in life's journey. When it gets rough and the enemy is blocking you from advancing, pray and ask God to show you who to call on for help. Ask for God to show you who is for you and who you can trust. It is imperative that you pray for discernment because not everyone on the team is a team player. Some have been set up in the camp to hinder you from fulfilling your purpose.

I pray that your eyes be open more spiritually and your ears more sensitive to God's voice. May God's blessings be your portion in great abundance.

Read Proverbs 27:17; Ecclesiastes 4:9-12; Galatians 6:1-2

What Are You Full Of?

There was a time in my life when I was full, but still felt empty. I was full of things that I thought would bring me satisfaction and fill the void in my life. I was full of lust, holding grudges, lies, cheating, idolatry, manipulation and confusion. To put it plain, I was living out my sinful pleasures. I gave my all only to be left feeling lonely, used up and unloved, full but still empty. When I accepted Jesus as Lord and Savior of my life, my eyes were opened more. My cry to God was and still is, Lord, I just want You! I became more aware of the things that I was allowing to have access to me and began to be filled with His attributes. It is a process, but I strive every day to be more like Him and now I'm living out my life to bring Him glory. What are you full of today?

Father I pray that you will fill and continue to fill all who seek to do your will. Let us never be empty, barren or lack any good thing you have for us. Remove everything that is not of your will for our lives and bless us to experience your fullness. Give us strength to resist the temptation we come up against. Bless us to see you in all that we go through, so that we won't be easily moved. Fill us up Lord. In Jesus name amen.

Read Galatians 5:16-25; Ephesians 5:17-18

It Is Harvest Time

I truly believe that we reap what we sow. I pray that God will release your plenty today. May you have plenty of joy, peace, resources, love, hope and whatever you need plenty of. I believe for God to release it to you in Jesus name!

Read Proverbs 11:24-25; Luke 6:38; 2 Corinthians 9:6-8; Galatians 6:7-9

God Will Use The Broken Pieces

My son and I were putting a puzzle together. We got to the end and had two spots left to fill. Well, one was missing, and the other one was damaged. I tried to convince my son that we could still use it, but he wasn't having it and insisted on throwing it to the side. He was crying and said, "Mom, we can't use it because it's broken."

All that you have been through in life is just another piece added to your puzzle. You're not too beat up to be used by God, in the end, you will be a complete work and beautiful to him. You're destined to fulfill His purpose for your life. Will you let Him put you back together?

Read 2 Corinthians 1:3-6; James 2:25

It May Not Come The Way You Think

I was watching this movie called, Moana, with my youngest two children. I don't agree with some of the content in the movie, but there's something that stuck out to me. Moana is traveling across the sea to find this god, to restore the heart of a god, who has the power to make the land flourish. She grew frustrated along the way and cried out to the sea for help. Shortly after a storm came, and her boat crash landed on an island. She began to express her frustration at the sea about how she asked for help and this is what it did. Little did she know that she was at the place she needed to be. I said all of that to say this. Sometimes we ask for God's help and guidance and he will send a storm to get us to our destination. We grow frustrated thinking that we've lost it all, but we've just arrived to where we need to be. Be encouraged through the storms of life. They are necessary for our growth and are often used to increase our faith. If you cried out to God for help and guidance, He does nothing short of that.

Read Jonah 1; Matthew 8:23-26; Romans 8:28

Lord, I Trust You

I've had my share of ups and downs in this life. One thing I can truly say is that, God has never failed me. Some things I've dealt with didn't go my way. Nonetheless I have learned that no matter what I go through, I must trust God. I encourage you all to do the same. Get up, hold your head up and keep your faith firmly in Him. So, despite what it looks like, don't lose hope in God, he's with you all the way. When you face the unthinkable say, Lord I trust you. When your backs up against the wall say, Lord I trust you. When people lie on you and turn their backs on you say, Lord I trust you. In the face of opposition say, Lord I trust you. Trust in the Lord, in Jesus name.

Read Job 13:15; Proverbs 3:5; Jeremiah 17:7

Just Ride

It's natural for us to want to know details, reasons why and where God is taking us in life. While there's nothing wrong with that, we must be careful of questioning God's decisions. We are limited to our understanding and will never fully know the mind of God and why He does certain things. If we say God is in control and we trust Him, why do we keep trying to take the wheel? Learn to let go, allow Holy Spirit to keep you buckled in position and trust God has you. Stop trying to figure out every turn, move and end point. Let God be God in your life.

Read Isaiah 40:13, 55:8-9

Too Much Too Late

In some instances in the Bible, God refused to answer the cry of his people. He would send a word of warning to them, but the people refused to take heed and ultimately suffered for their actions. There is nothing new under the sun. God is still speaking, and some people aren't taking heed. We can't live any way we want and expect to make it into heaven. The things were written in the Bible as an example to us. Don't ignore God and try to hustle at the last minute to get it right. Do it now, today, waiting could cost you your life. Don't wait another minute, because the next breath you think you're going to take isn't promised.

Read Proverbs 1:27-33; Luke 16:19-31, 17:26-30; Romans 15:4; 1 Corinthians 10:11; Hebrews 9:27

The Little Things Matter

I was fighting a sinus cold that had been lingering, which led me to feeling discouraged. I was sitting in class and could not focus, then suddenly I remembered that I had a cough drop in my pocket. I pulled it out and saw these words, "Push on!" and "Nothing you can't handle." I was taken back and could do nothing but praise God. I shut up my thoughts and stopped complaining. God used something as small as a cough drop to speak to me. Take time to pause, pay attention, pray and praise God for speaking to you, it doesn't matter who or what He uses to get our attention. If we're still enough, we'll see Him at work in all that we go through.

Read Numbers 22:27-28; 1 Corinthians 1:27

Remain Faithful

I was reading about Job and all that he endured. God allowed the devil to test Job with just about everything, but he couldn't kill him. In all the pain, hurt, loneliness, disappointments, sickness, loss and suffering that Job experienced, he remained faithful to God. Look at the life of Job, better yet Jesus, to give you encouragement through the ups and downs of life. While Job is a good example, Jesus is the greatest example, the only example we should follow. Don't let what you go through, cause you to turn your back on God. When man lets you down, remain faithful. When you lose all but your life and your mind, remain faithful. When you feel as if you can't anymore, remain faithful. If you're reading this, you're alive and still breathing. Give God praise right now and shout, God I will remain faithful. Remain faithful to God despite it all, he will reward you for your faithfulness. Hold on, keep on holding on.

Read 2 Chronicles 16:9a; Job 1:20-22; Hebrews 10:23; James 1:12

Leave It On The Altar, For Real This Time

There are some things that we've been entertaining that's not good for our spiritual well-being and is hindering us from fulfilling our purpose. As I was meditating, I heard the Lord say that I need to stop entertaining certain things because of the place He's taking me, they cannot go. Now, I didn't think these things were that bad but, God said that I must be living right, because the devil can recognize it. If we step to do the work of God and we're cutting up behind the scenes, the enemy will laugh in our face. We must stay dressed for war and stop playing, secretly sleeping with the enemy. All the mess that is contaminating our spirit man must go. God is calling for us to consecrate ourselves unto him. Now, I'm not saying be all holy to where you're no earthly good, but it's time to let go for real and be all in for the Lord. Leave these things on the altar and give God your all, not just some of you. We can't afford to be timid, shy or fearful when we're called to do something or living sinfully and expect for God to use us. Draw near to God, our very lives depend on our obedience in this move we're in.

Read Acts 19:13-16; 2 Corinthians 5:17

Change Me

We spend a lot of time focusing on the flaws of others. When we find ourselves doing this, we need to turn our eyes to ourselves and ask God to reveal what needs to be changed within us. As God shows you your flaws, humble yourself and pray for strength to change. None of us are perfect or have arrived at the place where we can condemn others. We all have some areas of improvement that needs work. When you begin to focus on yourself, what you see wrong in others won't look so bad anymore. Let the cry of your heart be, change me Lord.

Father I pray that you will change the way we think and see. Change how we respond and act. Change us until you're pleased with what you see. Do it Lord in the name of Jesus

Read Psalm 139:23-24; Lamentations 3:40-41;
Matthew 7:1-5

Fact, Faith or Feeling

At some point in our lives, we will come to a place where we will need to deal with the facts of life. If we allow our feelings to dominate our faith, we're in trouble. You see, the fact may be that you're facing an eviction. The fact may be that the doctor has given you a bad report. The fact may be that you're facing impossible odds and you're enduring hardships that seem too difficult to handle. Your feelings about it may be that you've been in this thing too long, and you're ready to throw in the towel. At the same time faith is saying, God will supply all my needs, I am healed, I am not alone because God is with me. Let your faith override your feelings and watch the facts change. The Lord knows your end from your beginning and it's sweet! I want to encourage you to not look at the now, walk by faith and claim your victory!

Read 2 Corinthians 5:7; Hebrews 11:6

When You Can't Think Your Way Out

One of the most challenging things for me to do, is to not try to figure out how things are going to work out. My mind is constantly trying to put things in order, and make sure that they run smoothly. When I get to the place where nothing is going the way I planned it, or I can't make sense of any of it, I tend to hit panic mode. This way of doing things is the total opposite of how God wants us to do them. We're not supposed to be thinking our way out, we must pray and trust Him. God will often move in ways that make absolutely no sense to us and he tells us not to worry about it. It is up to us to control how we respond to the trials and tests that we are faced with and who we decide to lean on is totally up to us. Will we lean to our way of thinking or lean on the Lord and trust for Him to provide and guide us through? Stop stressing about how it's going to work out, have faith and trust that it's already done. The things we face in life aren't sent for us to lose faith and give up. They're supposed to build us up and make us stronger. The real question is, will you let it?

Read Proverbs 3:5-6 and 16:9; Isaiah 55:8-9; Matthew 6:27, 33-34

The Great Exchange

We're sitting around here carrying burdens that don't belong to us. Walking around talking about it's in God we trust. If we trust God with it, then why do we stress so much? An exchange is when you give someone something in place of something else. So I ask, what have you given to God? Have you given Him your heart, in exchange for a clean one?

Have you given Him your life, in exchange for a new life? Or, are you exchanging hands with the enemy? God is the only one I know who can take the bad and make it good. He takes the burden and gives us rest. He gives us peace when we keep our minds on Him. Jesus laid down His life, paying the price for our sins, and in exchange we're redeemed and gain eternal life. This was, The Great Exchange. With Him, you can't lose. Give it up to God today, in exchange for something greater.

Read Ezekiel 36:26; Matthew 11:28-30, 20:28; 1 John 5:10-13

Follow God Every Step Of The Way

I was reading the story about when God told Abraham to sacrifice his son. 3 things came to my mind when I was reading it.

1- You can't always tell people what God said for you to do. I have yet to find anywhere it says that Abraham told his wife, or anyone what he was told to do. Imagine what their response would have been. You need to know the time to share, if at all. Some people will try to stop, or even steal and run with your vision.

2- We must go where God tells us to and do exactly what He says. What if Abraham would have gone to another place to offer up his son? Would the ram have been there? It's very imperative that we walk in total obedience to the Lord.

3- If you have children, continue to lift them up to the Lord. Abraham was willing to put his son on the altar and sacrifice him. His faith was so strong in God, he knew that He would provide. As we lift our children to the Lord, He will make provision for us.

Read Genesis 22:1-19

God Is More

God is more than just a feeling.
He is more than the goose bumps you get when you hear an inspirational song.
He is more than the stories you have heard about Him.
God is more than just a friend.
He is more than this life can give.
He is more than your bills paid.
God is more than the comfort offered by man.
He is more than the jobs we work.
He is more than we can even comprehend.
God is creator of heaven and earth.
God is love.
God is in control, even when things are out of control.
God is peace and joy.
God is the reason why we live.
God is all we need in this life to make it.
God is... Who is He to you?

God Is Faithful, Even When We Are Not

We all are subject to fall short of the glory of God. Therefore, we should never judge people and count them out when they fall. The same trap they are in, could very well be the one we ultimately slip into. What if your secret sins were revealed? How would you want people to treat you? What if God gave you what you deserved? We all have a past, so do not suppress people with your words and actions. Give a helping hand to those who are visibly struggling with sin and when you fall short, do not beat yourself up about it. If someone counts you out, remember whose opinion really matters about you, get up and keep trying. I went to the altar for prayer almost every week for the same thing and I didn't stop until I got delivered. I thank God that He didn't let me die in my mess and give me what I deserved. He was faithful even when I was not, and he forgave me when I sincerely repented. Thank you God for being faithful!

Read Psalm 86:15; Lamentations 3:22-23; Romans 3:3-4; Galatians 6:1-2; 2 Timothy 2:13

God Allowed It For A Reason

Have you ever heard the saying, no cross, no crown or, no test, no testimony? Some people want the blessings and benefits of being saved, but do not want to go through the fire. If we do not experience the challenging times, we may not really learn what grace is or experience His strength in our weakness. The difficulties of life are not too hard to handle. It is when we do not rely on God, and refuse to crucify our flesh, that it becomes a challenge to deal with. We will have joy, and we will have pain but after it's all said and done, our reward will be great. Lose your focus on the things of this life and turn it completely to God, so when difficult times arise, it will be easier to stay on course. Be encouraged in the Lord. God bless you!

Read Matthew 5:12; Romans 8:28; Colossians 3:1-3; 2 Timothy 4:8

Run With Patience

In this Christian race, we will face many different challenges. Some people will lie, cheat, steal and push you out of the way to get ahead. You will be offended and persecuted for no reason and may encounter those who claim to believe in God but are really wolves in sheep clothing. Not everyone who claims to know God does, you must learn how to use discernment and inspect the fruit of their lives. You will witness and experience a lot in this life but do not let it make you give up on God. When you love someone, you hold onto them and are willing to make sacrifices for them. God showed us that by sending his only Son as a sacrifice for our sins. He is with you in all that you do and go through in life. So be patient when it all seems to be falling apart and you do not see an end to it. Whatever is pulling on your patience, hold on and don't give up.

Read Philippians 4:6-7; Hebrews 12:1-3; James 1:2-4

Where Are My Sheep

My son was crying because he could not find this sheep game on his tablet. He kept saying, "My sheep, my sheep, my sheep!" God often speaks to me using natural events and as he was crying, I kept hearing my sheep, my sheep, where are my sheep? This is the question I believe that Jesus is asking us.

Some believers have wandered away from the truth and Jesus is calling out, looking for His lost sheep. He is also calling out to the ones who have not received Him. It is not God's desire that anyone die and go to hell. He gives us all free will and we choose how we want to live. If you are running, why are you? Is what you are doing worth you losing your soul and going to hell? If you have left, what caused you to leave the field? It is time to come back home.

Read Psalm 100:3; Jeremiah 3:13-15; Luke 15:3-7; 2 Peter 3:9

Don't Cry, God Heard You

I was in a deep sleep and was awakened by my baby calling my name. I immediately got out of the bed and picked him up. Then, I whispered in his ear, "It is okay, mommy is here, I have got you, now go back to sleep." He called my name a few more times, then he went back to sleep. This is what God does when we call on Him. He picks us up, reassures us that he is there and tells us to go back to sleep.

A lot of us are having sleepless nights and are not experiencing God's peace. Do not allow the enemy to deprive you of sleep and peace another day. Lay down, stop worrying and if by chance you need some aid, read the Bible. His Word is the best sleeping pill that you could ever take. God heard you and He has not forgotten about you. His timing is not ours, so just be patient and stand on his Word. Now, be at peace and go to sleep

Read Psalm 3:4-5, 4:8, 46:1; Proverbs 3:24; Matthew 11:28

When Your Fire Burns Down To A Small Flame

As you walk with the Lord, you will most likely experience a burn down. Some people call it a burn out, but I hear the Lord saying, it is just a burn down. The difference between the two is this; a burn out is something that is completely put out, while a burn down is when something is almost out. One thing I have learned is this, no one can put out the flame that God has sparked in you. When God puts it there, you have all you need to keep it going. Quit hanging around people and things that are trying to extinguish your fire. Get around people and things that are going to throw some spiritual accelerants on you. The enemy spits, sprays and even pours all he can on and at you to cause your fire to be put out. You cannot allow your passion and zeal for God to be dampened. Pull on God's strength to press your way through. How do you do this? Read, pray, fellowship, worship God, guard yourself, and exercise His Word in your life. Also, do not take on something that God has not said do. If the desire is still there, you have got something to work with. Even when you feel like giving up do not, let God complete the work He began in you.

Read Jeremiah 20:9; Acts 2:44-47; Philippians 1:6

Focus On God, Not Your Haters

At some point in your life, you will experience someone hating on you. You will also experience the betrayal of a friend. I used to cry about not having a lot of friends and it hurt when I found out that people did not like me. However, I have learned that I cannot please everyone, and some people just are not going to like me. I have also learned that you cannot buy friends. So, I choose to focus on what really matters; God, family, and the few true friends that I do have. We must stop wasting time and energy focusing on people who do not care and on those who left you. If we do not shift our focus off them, it will cause us to miss out on true happiness and fulfilling our purpose in life . Be kind to your haters and love them but do not allow them to take from you. If you desire companionship, ask God to help you to choose wisely those who will add value to your life. Your haters are always going to be in your midst, but God will teach you how deal with them.

Read Psalm 55:12-14, 56:11; Isaiah 26:3; Matthew 5:44-48

When God Says No

I accepted Jesus as my Savior when I was 18 years old and from that time until now, there has been some requests that I did not get. I cried and prayed, prayed and cried and nothing. For a moment, I thought that God was not listening to me or that I had done something wrong that was blocking me from Him. I thought that I would get everything I prayed for and that is not always true. You see, sometimes He will not give us what we want. When this happens, we cannot mistake His ability to do it with thinking He was not able to do it. I once heard that if you are not getting your prayers answered, then something is wrong with your faith or you are not praying right. Now, in some cases, our faith does need to rise but it could be that God is saying no or not yet. Instead of getting angry with God, ask him to allow you to discern his will when you pray. A lot of us do not know how to take rejection. If you are a parent or have children close to you, I am sure that at some point you have turned down a few of their requests. As our Father, God knows what is best for us, therefore he will not give us everything that we ask for. When He tells us no, it is for our own good, so do not get discouraged when things do not go your way. Learn how to work with what He allows and keep on moving. You will eventually see why He said no.

Read 2 Samuel 12:13-23; 2 Corinthians 12:7-10; James 4:2-3

God Speaks In The Dark Places

Have you ever been through so much, that you questioned your very existence? Or maybe for a moment, you thought about going back to your old ways because you felt like it was more fun and easier to live with. Being persecuted and going through hard times is inevitable. The Prophet Jeremiah went through major persecution for doing right. During one of his bouts in prison he got discouraged and began to question God. But, even in all that Jeremiah went through, God still spoke to him and used him greatly.

We can get in such a rut to where we feel as if we cannot take it anymore. I know because I have been there. When you find yourself there, count it all joy and praise God anyway. Your purpose is greater than the pain that you are experiencing. You need to see that everything you go through; God can use for his glory. It will all work together for the good. No matter how dark it is, the Light is with you and will lead you out. God is still speaking in the darkness, but are you too distracted to hear?

Read 1 Kings 19:8-18; Jeremiah 20:7-11

Enlarge Your Territory

When I was 22, I was single with 3 children to raise. I was unemployed and living back at home with my mom. I remember saying to myself, "If I get approved for this subsidized housing, then I will be set for life." I was limiting myself to accept the least that I could get. Please do not take this the wrong way, there is absolutely nothing wrong with getting assistance. What I am saying is, I used to think that was as far as I could go. I did not realize my dependence was on the system and not God. As I began to grow spiritually, I realized that there was more to life than just accepting the bare minimum. The help was never intended to be my main source, just a boost up to my next place.

Never limit yourself and settle for less. What people have to offer you is not supposed to replace what God can do. We must stop allowing the enemy to trick us into believing that this is all we are worth. God is limitless and wants us to experience the abundant life. I had to allow my faith to increase and my way of thinking to enlarge. Although it took years for some of the things to come, I kept speaking it and believing. Enlarge your territory and take the limits off of God.

Read 1 Chronicles 4:10; John 10:10

Selfless Life Selfless Love

Some disagreements we have in relationships is because we refuse to push our pride aside. We feel the need to vindicate ourselves and some of us will not rest until we get our point across. There is nothing wrong with being right and wanting gain but let Holy Spirit do his work and convict their hearts. Some of my greatest victories came when I remained silent. I sacrificed my need to speak and took it to God in prayer. We may hesitate to do this because it does not seem beneficial to us. However, we could end up missing blessings because of it. Ask yourself, how often do I really sacrifice myself for the better of others?

We must discipline ourselves to love and act beyond how we feel. True love makes sacrifices and sometimes giving it is not easy. You may have to give your time, money, commitment and some even sacrifice their lives. I am not telling you to neglect yourself for the wrong people and reasons. Let the Lord lead you and when He tells you to give, do it. It cannot always be about what you want. Let go of the all about me mentality and practice living a selfless lifestyle.

Read Isaiah 53:7; Matthew 27:12-14; John 15:12-13; Romans 5:7-8; 1 Corinthians 15:30-32; Philippians 1:20-26

Live Free Be Free

It is so easy to get entangled with the affairs of life. I often find myself engaging in this battle and wonder how the disciples and believers during their time made it. They saw Jesus face to face and witnessed His miracles but still struggled with their faith at times. The Word of God is our lamp and light. It will guide us through all we endure in this life. It may get worse before it gets better but be strong and stand firm on His Word. We have liberty in Jesus and must learn how to live free in Him. Relax your mind and think about His goodness. Think about how He sacrificed his life so that you can have life. Think about the countless times He delivered you and made a way. When you reflect on that, everything else will fade to the back. Then you will experience what it feels like to live free and be free.

Read Psalm 119:105; John 20:24-31; Galatians 5:1

From The Inside Out

I was slicing some potatoes and I cut my finger. I immediately went to the bathroom, cleaned and medicated it, then put on a band aid. One reason I did this was to keep it from getting infected. A couple of days had gone by and I looked to see how it was healing. A scab had begun to form inside of my finger, but the top layer was still open, and layers of my skin was coming back. Then I heard the Lord say, "From the inside out." I believe this how He desires to heal us.

Before we move forward into new relationships, ministries, jobs or whatever, we must allow time for healing. Our outward appearance seems fine and we groom it well, but the inside of us is torn into pieces. Because of this, we find ourselves in unproductive relationships, doing unproductive things and being unproductive with our time. Your wound became infected because you never let God fully clean, medicate and heal it. The good news is that it is not too late for God to do it. Let Him have his way so that you can be completely healed from the inside out.

Read Genesis 25:21; Job 5:17-18; Psalm 38:5; Hosea 6:1

Don't Miss Your Blessing Looking At The Crowd

My daughters' and I were out looking for deals on clothes. We went to one place and could not find anything. As we were pulling up to the second place, the girls said, "Mama, we are not going in there, it is way too packed and we are not going to find anything." At first, I was like maybe you are right and there is nowhere to park. But I could not shake the feeling that we were going to miss out on a blessing, so we went in anyway. We ended up leaving out with more than we imagined.

As you are seeking for things in life, do not look at the size, amount, or numbers. Just because it is big in number does not mean it is God or if it is small does not mean it is not God. These things do not matter to Him and he can use either for his will. Sometimes we miss out because we are too focused on the crowd. We fellowship based off size and find out it is not a place where God sent us. We must learn to be sensitive to Holy Spirit's leading and work with what He gives us. When you solely focus on God, numbers and size no longer matter.

Read Matthew 15:32-39, 18:19-20; Mark 5:25-29

Just Call On Jesus

I have been down so low that I could not look up. I have drifted away to the point I did not want to come back because of shame. I have offended people and did not care about how it made them feel. I denied Jesus in front of others because claiming Him was not the popular thing to do. I was walking in rebellion, too blind to see the consequences because I did not truly know God. But I am so grateful that in all I have done and even still do, He answers when I call.

No matter who or where you are, Jesus is just a call away. When you have gone too far and feel no hope, call on the name of Jesus. When you see no way out, call on the name of Jesus. When you feel left out, lonely and unloved, call on the name of Jesus. When you are fed up and at your wits end, call on the name of Jesus. When you cannot find the words to say, call on the name of Jesus. Just call on His name.

Read Psalm 18:6, 34:17-19; Romans 10:13

Why Won't This Giant Fall

I do not know about you but at times I feel the urge to scream. It is not that I do not believe or that I am mad, sometimes I get weak in this flesh and wonder, Lord how long? God will sometimes put things in front of us to get us where we need to be. The tests and trials create doorways of new opportunities for us. Not all giants are bad, and they will eventually fall. During these times, we are humbled and seeking God more fervently. I thank God for all my giants because they keep me pressing. The pressure keeps me praying and depending on God. If your giant has not fallen yet, be encouraged, do not give up and keep believing. It is going to come down.

Read Matthew 26:41; Philippians 1:12-13; Romans 8:28; 2 Corinthians 12:7-10; James 1:2-4

Lord, I Am Sorry

God sometimes speaks to me through my dreams. One morning as I was coming out of sleep, someone walked by me and asked, why did you stop? Some of us have experienced so much, it has caused us to abort our purpose and drift away from God. We should never allow anything cause us to fall off our posts. Whatever God has assigned for us to do is still in us and we are responsible for walking it out. He does not twist our arm and make us do it. The children of Israel wandered through the wilderness for years. They sinned, repented and God would forgive them, but most of them missed out on the promise. I am sorry was not cutting it anymore and God had to punish them. How many times have we prayed and cried, Lord I am sorry, and God forgave us? We cannot keep taking advantage of His kindness, he is a just God and we will have to answer for what we do. Do not miss out on the blessings He has to offer you. If you are sorry then you need to stop, actions speak louder than words.

Read Psalm 78:30-41; Matthew 15:8; James 1:22-23

The Simple Truth

If I asked a room full of people if they felt like they fall short of pleasing God daily, most of them would say yes. You see, some people have made it too complicated to keep up with God, when he is not that complicated. They have laid out all these stipulations, bylaws, and standards one must meet in order to be a part of the church. Now, do not take this the wrong way, standards need to be set, and things do need to be done in an orderly manner. It is when we make up our own set of rules apart from the Word, then we are wrong. It should not be a matter of meeting the requirements but rather what the condition of our heart and devotion to God is. If you love God, then true obedience will follow. He knew that we were not going to be good at keeping laws and rules. For this reason, He sent his Son to die for us so that our debt could be satisfied. Living a sanctified life can be a bit challenging at times. We need to stop beating up ourselves when we fall short of what is expected of us. Salvation is free and eternal life is promised to all who believe. It is our duty to fully surrender, obey God and love him with our whole heart, that is what you keep and meet. Believing the simple truth of His Word will free you from the spirit of failure and worthlessness.

Father free us from the guilt of not meeting what is required of us in Jesus name.

Read Ecclesiastes 12:13-14; Matthew 22:37; John 14:15; Galatians 3:19-29; Ephesians 2:8-10; Colossians 2:8

Broken And Changed

My husband and I were talking about the children starting school. At the time, our son, CJ, was three years old and had a very unhealthy sleeping pattern. He slept in until about twelve in the afternoon and would go to sleep between twelve and four a.m. I said the first thing that needed to happen was his sleeping pattern needed to be broken and then it can be changed. This is just what we experience spiritually, we get broken down and then God works on changing us.

Do you have some unhealthy ways that need to be broken or are you going through the broken process? The broken place can be lonely, painful and difficult, but is necessary for rebuilding. Sometimes God will strip us bare to break the habits and sinful desires we have. It is designed to humble us and bring us to a place of full surrender to Him. Allow God to do his work in you so that his will can be perfected in your life.

Read Jeremiah 18:1-4; James 1:2-4

A Good Spanking

Some of what we are experiencing is just flat out discipline. Most of us when we are wrong do not admit it right away. It can be that we do not see it because the enemy has blinded us by pride, we were trained that way, or we know to do right and just refuse. Whatever the reasons are, it needs to be addressed and corrected. If you have children or individuals you oversee, you are only going to allow so much. The time will come when you will need to address the issue and punish them. In doing this you are showing them that you love them. So, when God returns the same to us, we need to take it. It does not feel good when you get spanked and you do not see the benefits at the time. All of us at some point will experience God's rod of discipline. How will you respond when it comes?

Read Proverbs 13:24; Hebrews 12:5-11

Flawless Leaders? Flawless Church?

The day I accepted Christ into my heart was the best day of my life. This decision shaped me in ways I never thought were possible. When I first got saved, I did not know what to expect. I believed every word preached and in everyone who was a fellow brother or sister. In the first several years of my walk, I experienced things that caused me to slowly drift away from the church. I was confused and hurt but God did not allow me to stay in that place. He sent people into my life that ministered to me and helped me get back on track.

We sometimes make the mistake of putting too much trust and confidence in people, and when they fail us, we fall off. If you are looking for the perfect leader or perfect church, you will not find one. Someone once told me that if it was a perfect church, it stopped being so when I walked through the door. We all have some areas that need improved. The only perfect leader to ever walk the earth was Jesus Christ. The perfect church is not going to be experienced until we are living eternally with Him. Now that you know there is no perfect place or people, go back, get fed the Word, and get busy helping build up His kingdom. God bless you!

Read John 14:2-4; Romans 3:23; Ephesians 5:1; 1 John 2:6; Revelation 21:1-4

True Marks Of A Christian

When the early church began, some believers were putting emphasis on being circumcised and keeping the law. The Apostle Paul debated a lot about this and taught that it is not outward deeds but inward deeds from the heart that really matters. We have gotten so focused on the outside and making ourselves look and sound good, while the inside of us is rotting away. The true marks of a believer are noticed from the inside out. You can hold to all the rules of your local fellowship and dress well but still be on your way to hell. What is the condition of your heart today? How are you treating the people around you and those who come to your place of fellowship?

Read Romans 2:29; Galatians 6:11-18

Destined To Be Loved

Before you were born, God knew all that you would do but still chose to love you. His love was put in flesh form, Christ Jesus, and died on the cross for our sins.

No matter where you are and what you have done, God still loves you.

Read John 3:16-17; Romans 5:6-8, 8:38-39

If You Sow You Will Reap

Some days I feel like I am running on empty. I give without restraint and afterwards barely have enough for myself. The enemy sometimes taunts me and says, look at all you do and for what, to still struggle? The temptation to fall into this trap is strong but I remind myself of what God said and I stand on that.

Some of us have sown for years and have yet to see the harvest. We have given much and taken little or nothing in return. Do not give up being a giver. God's Word is true and cannot be taken back. Eventually we will reap what we have sown and what we have been promised is going to come. But we are not exempt from going through challenges in this life. When we do, God will give us just what we need to make it. Keep waiting and keep believing, our time is coming!

Read Matthew 4:3-4; Luke 6:38; Romans 3:4; Galatians 6:7-10

Was It A God Move?

Some of us have made impulse moves based off how we feel. We move after an offense, to get away from the drama. We move for lack of love and feeling unappreciated. We move for the money, hoping it will be the answer to our financial woes. Whatever decision you have made and later found out it was not God, that is what I am talking about. However, if we take heed, we can learn something from these moves. God can use these moves to humble us and mature us spiritually. Someone told me a quick move is not a God move and in some cases that may be true. We must seek God for direction, be patient and do not move based off our feelings. We need to be sensitive to time and purpose. There is saying, "the grass ain't always greener on the other side". Some of us got there and found out this was true. But understand this, if it was a God move, change is soon to come. Be still and listen.

Read Psalms 37:23; Proverbs 16:9

Surviving The Scandal

Have you ever been shot down with words by people? Have you ever felt confused because you did not see immediate results, after obeying God? Have you ever stood up for good and was persecuted? At some point in our lives we will endure these things and more. The prophet Jeremiah spoke a message that was rejected by most all the people, despite that he continued to obey God. The Apostle Paul killed Christians and persecuted the church before his conversion. Can you imagine how that conversation went after he got saved and started preaching?

It seems as if our sensitivity to such things is magnified after salvation. Why is that? In my opinion, we just do not expect for certain people to mistreat us, especially those of the faith. The enemy often attacks from the inside out. We must develop a tolerance to the point that it does not affect our personal lives and walk with Christ. After it is all said and done, the only thing that matters is if God is pleased. People will scandalize your name even after you are gone. Only in Christ will we find the strength to overcome when we are faced with these things. You are who God says you are!

Read Jeremiah 26:8-15; Acts 9:1-2, 10-16, 19-22

Who Dropped You?

God never intended for people to carry us throughout our whole journey with him. We are only to be carried for so long and then we are put down so we can walk on our own. We grow in God, get off our spiritual crutches and walk by faith. We can no longer sit and sulk about who dropped us and who hurt us. At some point we must learn to lean totally on God, not people. We are putting too much dependence on man, expecting for them to do what only God can do. No one is perfect and people will fail you. When they do, do not worry about it, use that experience to build up on instead of allowing it to destroy you. Whoever dropped you was supposed to because you were too big for them to continue carrying. Dropping you did not kill you, it saved you.

Read 2 Samuel 4:4; Psalm 118:8; Proverbs 3:5-6; Ephesians 6:10

Aborted Purpose

When I was pregnant with my son, the specialist we were seeing suggested that we abort the pregnancy. When my husband and I heard this, it was crushing, but something in me would not let me accept that. I looked her in the eyes, and I said, "We appreciate all you have done, but we will not have any further testing and we are going to trust God on this."

The enemy has sent certain people on assignment to speak death into your purpose and vision. If God gave it to you, that is all you need to see it through to fruition. Our son is happy, busy and healthy as can be by God's grace! Stop allowing what people say and what you think cause you to abort your purpose. I speak life into every one of your dreams, ministries and visions! Rise up and let it live!

Read Genesis 21:9-21; Isaiah 55:11

Too Busy To Worry

Most of us are overwhelmed with the responsibilities of life. We are constantly on the go, and sometimes miss out on the things that are important. We get so caught up worrying, it takes away our joy in living. I believe that when we get busy about doing God's will, we will not have time to worry about the other stuff and our joy will be filled. We can find a rest and contentment in God that will free our minds of the cares of this world. I cannot explain why or how this completely works, but it does. God is just awesome like that! I have found that when I focus on God more, my stress levels subside and anxiety leaves. When your mind focuses on God things change, and good habits will follow. So, get in the habit of serving and loving God and as you do this, watch how things change in your life.

Read Matthew 6:33; Philippians 4:8-9; Colossians 3:2

How Bad Do You Want It?

My toddler son was misbehaving and as I went to get him, he intentionally jumped in-between the couch and the wall. Unfortunately, he ended up getting stuck and had to call on me to help him out, but I could not see him because he was too low. The more desperate he became, the more he pushed and eventually he was able to reach up for me. He came up just enough for me to grab him out. The moral of the story is this.

Sometimes we disobey God, run and try to hide from him. When we do this, we often get stuck in places that we find hard to get out of. We call on Him to help us out, but nothing happens right away. God is merciful and long suffering, so he will not leave us there. It is not until we want it bad enough and take the initiative to come out that He helps us. If you want it, you may have to work for it. God works with the willing, sometimes you will need to do your part to be free.

Read 2 Kings 5:10-14; Matthew 4:17; Romans 10:9-10

Unrestricted Time

How many times have you gotten discouraged while waiting on God to deliver you? Then after a period of waiting and stressing about it, He works it out for you. Our minds will never fully comprehend God and why he chooses to do certain things in our lives. Do not allow your mind to stay thinking negatively. God does not move by our time and he often goes against all logic. He works out the impossible to man. Your situation is a mishap to you but to God it is your next step up to your breakthrough. He had to allow this to humble you and bring you to a place where you solely rely on him. The process can be mind-boggling and long, but keep in mind that God is on unrestricted time. Keep holding on and trust the process of His time.

Read Psalm 27:14, 90:4; John 11:1-4, 39-45

Aim Your Works Toward God

It is natural for us to want recognition for our achievements and when it does not happen, it leaves us feeling unappreciated. That feeling is far from true when it comes to God. He loves us and wants to use us. When we aim to please Him and do it out of a sincere heart, he honors that. So, if your good deeds and works go unnoticed by people, that is okay. Keep in mind it is God you are working for, not man. When you do all things as unto Him, your labor will get easier to bare. Now, I am not telling you to not stand up for yourself, because people will take advantage of you. Keep your focus on God in all you do and watch him change things on your behalf.

Read Philippians 2:13-15; Colossians 3:17, 22-24

No Pain No Gain

Do you remember playing arm wrestle and when you were about to lose how the pain dropped you to your knees? Or when someone twisted your arm behind your back and made you say uncle? Well, this is what often happens in the spirit realm. The enemy wrestles against us attempting to make us fall into sin. However, when we stand our ground, his attempts fail, and God uses it for our good. The good is that the pressure causes us to pray and admit our dependence on God. Stop wasting your breath on saying the devil caused this or that. Instead, give God the glory and call on Him every time you get in a struggle. You need to believe that God is going to use your pain to bring about your gain.

Lord I pray you bless us to see that our pain has a purpose and all things lead to the glory of you. In Jesus name, amen.

Read Romans 8:28; 1 Peter 3:14-17

Miracle Worker

We are living in some very trying times that leaves some to question the existence of God. I heard the Lord say, you do not have to know how I am going to make the way, only trust and believe I am a Miracle Worker. Whatever you are going through do not give up and lose hope. Be strong and be bold in your faith. God has already made the provision for you and nothing is impossible when it comes to Him. You do not need to know how He is going to do it, just believe that he is.

Read Luke 1:37

Just Laugh

Sometimes we will need to laugh to keep from crying. When it appears that the enemy is winning, be joyful and thank God for each day he blesses you to see. The Bible says that God laughed at his enemies when they thought they had the upper hand. He knew something that they did not, and they would all soon taste defeat. So as your enemies are enjoying what they see as defeat, sit back and laugh at them. God will deal with them and they will be stopped.

Read Psalm 37:12-13

Embrace The Rain

The storms in your life have been pouring down and you feel as if there has been no relief. You may be wondering when it will stop, I hear the Lord saying, "Now!" The rain is only fertilizing the seeds that have been planted over the years and your harvest is getting ready to spring up. There is a harvest of plenty coming to your house. Embrace the rain and lay hold on the promises of God, it is so!

Read 1 Kings 18:41-46

Broken Faith

Has something happened that has caused your faith to be shattered? Maybe you have lost a loved one, or your breakthrough seems to be taking forever. We are not exempt from experiencing hurt and challenging times. Whatever has caused your faith to be broken, take it to the Lord and ask him to restore your faith. Our faith will be tried, and we must press hard to keep it during those times. Do not allow your heart to become bitter against God. His timing is not our timing and his will is sometimes hard for us to accept. Put your heart back into the hands of God and trust him again. He loves you with unconditional love. He will never fail, nor has he left your side.

Read Matthew 21:21-22; Luke 22:31-32; Hebrews 11:1,6; 1 Peter 1:6-7

Fixed Fight

I was ear hustling at work as my coworkers were discussing the basketball play offs. I chimed in and said, it is fixed so why are you all arguing about it? Then the thought came to me, fixed fight. It does not matter how much of an advantage the enemy appears to have; we have already won. You may be down right now, but it is not over! Things are not really what they appear to be, and you are not fighting with people. You are fighting our enemy, the devil, on a spiritual battleground. You cannot fight him using natural techniques, you must use your spiritual weapons to fight him back. Go to God in prayer and war there, it works.

Read 1 Corinthians 15:57; 2 Corinthians 4:8-9, 10:3-6; Ephesians 6:11-18; Philippians 4:6-7

Reveal Remove Restore

It is my personal prayer that God continues to reveal, remove and restore me. The process goes like this;

Reveal: Once God reveals our issues, we are held accountable to change. He gives us free will therefore giving us an opportunity to make the right decisions.

Remove: When God reveals our flaws, we need to ask him to give us strength to let go and fully surrender to him so that he can remove the flaws.

Restore: Whenever something is taken away or broken down, there is a need for restoration. Pray for God to restore you and fill every vacant place so that the enemy has nowhere to return.

Read Psalm 139:23-24

Joy

The enemy has come and zapped some of us of our joy. The Word of God tells us not to let anything take our joy away, so why are we walking around joyless? The enemy comes for no other reasons but to destroy us and he tries to get us to focus on our problems. Let us not allow the devil another day where he does not belong. Put Jesus back in his rightful place in your life and you will experience His J.O.Y.

Jesus
Over
Your feelings!

Read John 10:10, 15:11, 16:22

Will You Still Believe?

We are living in times where our faith is being put to the test. Life's circumstances are tempting us to question if we really believe. It had to be difficult for Moses to believe that God was going to part the Red Sea and swallow up their enemies. Let us not forget when Abraham was told to sacrifice his son, that had to take some serious faith. It is difficult to have faith while in the fire. However, when we realize that God is with us, the feeling of doubt fades away. We must keep believing even though it seems impossible to beat and we cannot see a way out. If God decides not to give us what we desire, do not think He was not able to, God can do all things. It is not a question of His ability to do it but rather if it is His will for your life.

Read Genesis 22:1-3; Exodus 14:15-18; Daniel 3:16-18; Hebrews 10:38

Trust Me

I was reflecting on some recent things that have taken place and I started to question why. After a few minutes of sitting there, I heard the Lord say, "Trust Me." I have been told that the Lord will bless us to understand better by and by. I believe that after a season of testing, He will do just that. When you cannot seem to understand why and are not sure what to do, stand on the promises of God. There is a reason He is allowing these things to happen in your life. You do not know why, and God may never reveal it to you. We must learn to trust Him despite the things we go through in life. Stand your ground and say, Lord I trust you.

Read Job 13:15, 36:26; Proverbs 3:5-6

Deny, Do And Don't

In order to be more effective in our walk with Christ, we need to learn how to exercise these three things.

Deny: In order to follow Christ, we must deny ourselves and surrender to Him. One way we do this is by letting go of what we want and ask Him what he desires from us.

Read Matthew 16:24

Do: We must be willing to obey Him and sometimes this can be a bit of a challenge. I say that because most people do not want to be pressed and crushed. We must be willing to obey God regardless how difficult it seems. If you love Him, you will do as He says.

Read Matthew 19:21-22; John 14:15

Don't: You cannot move forward and stay focused if you are constantly looking back. Stop allowing your past to drain you of your present passions. It can potentially kill you and stall you from fulfilling your purpose. So, do not look back!

Read Genesis 19:24-26; Luke 9:62, 17:31-32

Don't Give Up

When I surrendered to the Lord, all I knew at the time was that I needed change. I was unaware that this road would take me on such an emotional journey; I had not counted the cost of my yes. The best decision that you can ever make is submitting your life to the Lord. But with that decision comes a lot of work on your behalf to keep on the path. Count it all joy and do not give in to the lie that you made the wrong choice. The road may get hard, but God will be with you every step of the way. Hold up your head and be encouraged in the Lord.

Read Joshua 24:15; Luke 14:28; Philippians 2:12

God Has Not Forgotten About You

It may seem as if you have hit the bottom and there is no redemption. What you are feeling is far from the truth because God loves you and he cares. If you have breath and a will to be obedient to the Lord, it is not too late for you. His arms never closed; he is waiting for you to come back. The time is now for you to run back to the Lord, now go!

Read Luke 15:17-21, 32

Know Who You Serve

As I was preparing this thought, I was praying about how I should say it. Some of us are sitting under the wrong leadership. We have been stagnant and wonder why we have not had much growth. Often, we will only go as far as they go. It is imperative to know the heart of our leader because whatever qualities and characteristics they possess, we are subject to having the same. Just like we are known by the company we keep; we are known by the leadership we sit under. We develop their habits and traditions, so we must be careful of who feeds us. Know your leader, and do not be afraid to confront them in love if they are out of order. It is time for us to be real and hold those who lead accountable.

Read 1 Samuel 3:10-19 Luke 6:39-40, 17:3

Don't Lose Sight

We cannot get caught up in victories that God gives us on earth to where we miss the greater reason to shout. Do not lose sight of what and where it is you have been promised to inherit, eternal life in heaven with the Father. This world is not our home, our home is heaven, there is no place like home.

Read John 14:1-4; Philippians 3:20-21; Colossians 3:2-3

Suffering In Silence

My three-year-old son was in the bathroom washing his hands, and I heard a low whimper. I went to check on him and noticed that his face was frowned up, and his head was down. I asked him what was wrong, but he refused to answer me, so I had to play the guessing game to figure it out. The lesson is this, pride can cause a delay in your healing and deliverance. Not everyone can see into your situation to know what is going on with you. The first step to getting help is to tell someone about your problem and ask for help. God did not put you here for you to go through alone, He has placed people there to help you. Stop suffering in silence and speak up so that you can be free.

Read Exodus 18:17-24; Proverbs 16:18; Mark 10:51-52; Romans 12:5

Don't Die In The Dry Place

The children of Israel were taken into bondage because of their disobedience. While there, God sent a word to them saying, build, multiply in number and make the best of their time there. The Lord knew that it was not the end for them.

It may seem like you have reached the end of the road, and there is nothing good left to experience. If God blessed the children of Israel while they were in bondage, why would He not do the same for you? Do not die in your desert place. I hear the Lord saying, there is a spring of living water there. He is that spring of living water, focus on Him and live! It will not always be like this. Start taking joy in the little things. If you are reading this, that means you are still alive, and God is not through with you yet. Get up and live!

Read Jeremiah 29:4-6; John 4:10-14; Hebrews 13:8

Trust The Process

Fear is often our first response to trouble or a trying situation. However, we cannot allow ourselves to stay there, we must set our focus on God. Some of us are in a season of divine alignment and the shift has already begun. It is imperative that we trust the process. God has control over every detail of our lives. Give all your cares to Him, have faith and wait.

Read 2 Chronicles 20:1-4; Proverbs 16:9; Romans 8:28

Write It Down

Write down your visions, dreams and goals when you receive them so that you will not forget them. I believe that when we reflect on what we write, then we relive the moment and reality of it sets back in. These feelings spark revival inside of us and the passion for it is rekindled. Do not give up on what you are believing God for. If it is part of His plan for you it will come to pass. Write it down so you can see it and reflect on it. Doing this will keep your hope up for it and get you through until it manifests.

Read Jeremiah 36:2-3; Habakkuk 2:1-4

Don't Flee When You Can't See

Some of us have gone into hiding. We have allowed fear and frustration to get the best of us and retreated due to the pressure. The truth is you cannot hide from God, and you can only run for so long. There was a time in my life that I would run at the first sight of mess. I would not confront the problem or stick around to see if it would work out. Now understand this, God will allow your waters to be troubled to get you to move, but there are times when He wants us to be still and endure the process. Resist the urge to flee when the pressure is turned up. It is not a time to run rather a time to pray, confront our problems and endure the process of coming out. We must follow His lead out of the place we are in and move by faith. Stand firm in the place God has you to be and know it is well.

Read 1 Kings 19:1-3; Jonah 1:1-4; 2 Corinthians 5:7

Don't Get Hooked On Looks

God can use anyone he chooses to deliver a message and fulfill his purpose. I am reminded of the time when I was unwed and pregnant. I had repented of my wrong and was doing my best to live right for God. My pastor, another minister and I went to visit a lady who had been in a bad car accident. As we were leaving, God told me to tell her not to blame herself. I shared that because I want you to know that God will not always use people who look, live, act or smell like how we think they should. Receive the message and embrace the messenger, do not miss it by looking at the package. They could be holding the blessing you have been waiting for.

1 Samuel 16:1, 7, 11-13; Isaiah 53:2; Matthew 3:1-6

No Condemnation

We sometimes beat up ourselves over the decisions we have made. Whether the decisions cost us much or little, God is saying, "No condemnation." We must learn how to let go and forgive ourselves of the things that has caused us grief. Despite what you have done, God knew beforehand. The fact of the matter is if you are still breathing, forgiveness is available to you. God is merciful, he is not as harsh as some think he is. Our minds will never be able to comprehend the depth of His love for us. Stop condemning yourself and rise from your place of pity. Receive God's love and forgiveness.

Read Psalm 103:8-14; Romans 8:1; 1 John 1:9

Put It Away

If the enemy could have his way, you would never be free from his grips. But to God be the glory his power has been broken! Once we become knowledgeable of God, we have a weapon that cannot be overthrown, his Word. We must learn how to use His Word to overcome the pressures of life and the tactics of the enemy. When the offender rises, you must shut him down immediately. You need to cast down every negative thought and free yourself of sinful habits. Also, put away the things that have held you down and kept you locked up in your mind. Let go of the negative views of life and embrace all things in the light of Christ.

Father in the name of Jesus I pray that you will bless us to cast down every way of thinking, doing and speaking that is contrary to your will. Bless us to take another look and this time to see it through the eyes of faith. Give us the strength we need to overcome every challenge and let go of every weight that has been holding us down. Bless us to be encouraged and I thank you for doing it for us. In Jesus name amen.

Read Ephesians 4:22-32; Philippians 4:8-9; Hebrews 12:1

His Hand Is Not Too Short

I heard someone say, "If God has to reach way down, he will pick you up." I did not understand what that meant until I fell off and felt like God did not care. I thought that He was going to leave me there in my backsliding ways. I felt unworthy of His forgiveness and thought I was too far gone to come back to him. I did not think His grace was enough and thought his mercy had been cut from me. The enemy had me isolated and in a place of pity. The longer I dwelled on the negative thoughts, the deeper I fell into his traps. But I am so glad that the way I was feeling was a lie. It was not permanent, and God's grace had not run out. He still loved me and cared about my well-being. I learned that God's hand is not short, and He can pick up and clean up the worst of us. So, if you have found yourself stuck in that place, know there is hope; that hope is the Lord! He will never leave you and his grace and mercy has not run out on you. If you are reading this that means He is still working on your behalf and has given you another chance. May you embrace His love and find all you need in him.

Read Deuteronomy 30:4; Psalm 18:16; 1 Timothy 1:12-16

Mask Off

It is my opinion that a lot of us in the church have masked religion. Looking from the outside, it appears that everything is good and functioning optimally. I had a vision of a scab and at the first glance, it looked like healing had taken place. Then suddenly puss began to pour out of it. God told me that this was the condition of the church, we have ignored the symptoms of the infection for too long. We have become too timid to address in love the sin for fear of opposition. We have mastered a good shout and embraced the entertainment of those that mount the pulpit service after service. It is time that we begin to be honest with ourselves, and really dig deep to get to the surface of our own issues. The cover up can only last for so long, then the truth will be revealed. It is time that we take off the mask and allow God to heal us from the inside out. We must begin to deal with the things that are plaguing the church and stop allowing things just because we want a good service. When we do that, I believe that true deliverance and healing can begin to take place.

Read Matthew 7:22-23; 1 Corinthians 5:6; Revelation 3:1-3

How Are You Handling The Presence Of God In Your Life?

As I look at the condition of the church today, this question came to my mind. How are we handling the presence of God? It is recorded in the Bible how the people feared the Lord, and literally could not stand in His presence. Some even died if they mishandled what represented God's presence and died when lying in his presence. Today there seems to be little to no reverence for the Lord, and a lack of understanding of how powerful His presence is in our lives. Some people fear more when they sin in front of the pastor, negligent to the fact that God is everywhere and knows all things. It is my prayer that we will become more serious about the things of God. I pray that we would make more conscious decisions to live right and stop making excuses for why we sin. It is time we start giving God more respect and reverence and handle with care his presence in our lives.

Read Numbers 4:15; 2 Samuel 6:2-7; Acts 5:1-11; 2 Corinthians 4:7; Hebrews 12:28-29

Mishandled Grace

I wrestled with whether or not I was going to be open about this, but how else to be free unless you release it. A few years ago, my home went into foreclosure. I was very selective about who I told, because I know how people can be. The past several years, have been nothing short of challenging for my family. One day I was discussing my financial situation with someone and I was asked, "If you can pay over one thousand dollars for rent, how in the world did you lose your house?" Almost immediately the words mishandled grace came out of my mouth. You see, I would take advantage of the grace period I was given to pay my mortgage payment. I had done it for years until the bank finally decided enough was enough, and they denied me another modification. I was filled with so many mixed emotions, but I could only blame myself. Had I done things in order of priority things would have been different. But even in that I remained confident that God works all things together for my good even when it is my fault. All I am trying to say is, do not mishandle the grace God is giving you. So many things can be prevented if we take heed and act right. Take into consideration the time you have been given and always be willing to share His Word with others. If He has convicted your heart and said repent, do it now while you still have breath on this side. Be very careful not to mishandle the grace of God.

Read Judges 16:20-21; Psalm 90:12; Romans 6:1-2; 2 Peter 3:8-11

Faith Under Fire

I went through a season where it seemed as if all my streams had dried up. I exhausted every resource, and all my crutches were removed. Some things came from direct decisions that I made, and some things just happened. Through it all, I learned to not lean on my way of doing things and to praise God despite my problems. I learned how to put out negative thinking and embrace my faith in God. One of the most important things I learned was patience. I had to learn how to be content with little to nothing, while yet believing God for everything.

Read Philippians 4:11; 1 Timothy 6:6-8; James 1:2-4

Push Back And Push Up Your Praise

When your backs up against the wall do not fall, press and pray. The enemy desires for you to keep silent because he knows the power that comes forth when you speak, especially when under pressure. I hear the Lord saying, "If you would just open your mouth, I am waiting to hear from you, you are right where I want you to be." Do not get weary, God is with you and relief is on the way, so hang on. Press pray and praise God all the way through it; there will be glory after this.

Read Psalm 34:17-19; Romans 8:18

This Will Not Break Me!

As I was meditating on the goodness of the Lord, I heard him say, "Be still and see the salvation of my hand at work in your life." If I could tell everything that I am going through, some would question why I have not turned back. I just have enough faith to believe that God can do anything. Even when things do not work out the way that I think they should, I remain confident in Him. I cannot allow my challenges, tests or trials to shake or move me. I will speak His Word and have faith despite how I feel or how it looks. Stand firm on His promises because you will come out on top. I declare that we will no longer walk in defeat and doubt that God is able! No longer will the enemy trick us into believing his lies! No longer will we say, we cannot make it! I declare with the authority of the power of God within me that this will not break us in Jesus name! The name above all names and the name by which we have our liberty and power!

Read Job 42:1-2; Psalm 55:22; Jeremiah 32:27; Ephesians 3:20-21

Crunch-Cry-Calm

I was reading out of a Teen Bible I bought a few months ago. There was a small section that said, Israel sinned, was punished, they cried out to God and he saved them. I immediately began to reflect on my past and the many times God has delivered me.

The Crunch- This is a period of time when we suffer for the mistakes we have made, sin or from the inevitable events that take place in our lives.

The Cry- These are times when we cry out to God from our broken and desperate places, when we feel lost, confused or frustrated.

The Calm- The overwhelming sense of peace that God brings after you have suffered for a little while. The feeling of freedom when you have been delivered from what once held you bound.

I challenge you to remember God's patterns over the span of your life. Has He not brought you out before? Has He ever left you alone? Be encouraged despite the season you are in. Your cries have reached His ears and he will deliver you.

Read Exodus 2:23-25; Psalm 34; 1 Peter 5:10

The Lord Will Not Leave You Broken And Bound

There have been times where I felt like I had no energy to keep pushing. I took blows and ridicule for both doing right and doing wrong. What I have found is that no matter the reason, they both have similarities with regards to how it made me in those seasons of brokenness. I have also found that God is always with me and will deliver. I may have had to lose some stuff in the process, but it was for my benefit and brought me closer to Jesus. The trying times you are facing right now are meant to draw you into God's loving arms. He wants us broken so we can see our need for Him. He allows for us to experience being bound so that we can know what it is to be free. Seek God in your broken and bound place. Then, after you have done all you can and know to do, be still and rest in Him. Let His Word transform your mind, so that you can truly experience his peace. He will never leave you broken and bound.

Read Deuteronomy 31:6; Psalm 34:17-19; Isaiah 26:3; Jeremiah 29:11; John 8:36

No Matter How Heavy The Load, You Must Carry It

As I was packing and loading up my car, I looked down and I saw an ant carrying a flying insect. The other bug was much larger than the ant, and I am assuming stronger as well. I watched as the ant dragged it across the ground until it hit a leaf with a stem and got stuck. The ant struggled but refused to let go of the bug and kept going until it got over the leaf. God gave me a revelation in that. It does not matter how heavy the load gets in your life, your will to survive must be stronger. You need to press when no one else is there to help you carry the load. You must patiently endure the storm and keep going on no matter what. God will sometimes speak to us using simple things, but we need to be still and listen.

Read Proverbs 6:6-8; Luke 9:23; Philippians 3:14

Get Out The Way

We have all at some point experienced something that has made us question God. Truth is that despite how much we question Him or try to figure him out, we will never fully understand. I am the type of person who needs to have it all figured out, at least that is what I thought. I was facing a problem I could no longer mask, and I had to watch as it all came crumbling down. I had to face the hard reality that it was beyond my control and I could not fix it. I failed to realize that some of my struggle was because I was trying to be in control of things. I thought that my way made more sense and was more beneficial. I had to stop fighting against the inevitable and let God take the reins for real. I speak the truth when I say that it was not an easy thing to do. However, I knew that God had me right where he wanted me, a place of full surrender to Him. A place where my only way out was through Him. I encourage you to make a conscious effort to get out of the way of what God is doing in your life. Then, be still and be patient while He is working.

Read Numbers 22:32-34; Ecclesiastes 3:11; Isaiah 55:8-9; Romans 11:33-34

Pruned To Perfection

These last few years have presented various challenges in my life. I can respond one of two ways, praise God or complain about it. I have learned that complaining about things will not get you very far. When you allow God to work his process in your life, you will experience his peace. You will learn that even if it does not change, you change for the better. You will see that all along God was trimming you of the fat in your life to make you 'lean' on Him. What is happening is not sent to take you out, you are just being pruned to perfection. Keep allowing the Master Gardener to prune your garden.

Read Proverbs 3:5-6; John 15:1-2

It's In My Weakness

The tests and trials I have experienced initially had me feeling alone, confused, frustrated, and almost to the point of giving up. It was so bad that I thought about retreating and isolating myself from everyone, then God spoke to me. He reminded me that this was no strange place because I had been here before, and it was an attempt of the enemy to bind me again. The noise of complaints was loud in my head, but I had to choose to listen to the soft and calm voice of the Lord. When I did this, I began to feel like jolts of energy surge through me and giving up was no longer an option. His Word began to come out of my mouth, and praise followed. At first, I tried to suppress it because I felt like what is the use, but it was irresistible. In that moment I realized that His presence is even more strong when I am weak. It was in my weakness that I found Him to be a present help. It was in my weakness that I realized just how equipped He made me to handle the pressures of life. It was in my weakness that I learned to lean on Him, and not my own understanding. It was in my weakness that I found Him to be all I needed and more.

Read Psalm 46:1; 2 Corinthians 12:8-10

Just A Little Love And Patience

The thought of giving up is often the first thing that comes to our minds when we hit challenging times. Whether at home with family, the church or at work, our patience will be tested. It is very challenging to be patient with someone who is being used to test you. However, it is during these times that we are given the opportunity to let the love of Christ show through our actions. When you think about how much God loves you, and is patient with you, you will find it easier to show others the same grace. We must stay humble and realize that we did not mature overnight. We must keep in mind that we are not perfect and never will be. Someone had to put up with our nasty ways until God delivered us. Think about this, if God's patience ran out on you where would you be? So, learn to be patient with people and love them; a little goes a long way.

Read Ephesians 4:2-3; Colossians 3:12-17; 2 Timothy 2:24-26

The Fog

There are moments when you will feel lost and confused and cannot make sense of anything. You will want to give up and will be overwhelmed with the thoughts of why me, what am I going to do and how will I make it. The fact is that God does not always allow for us to see the full picture nor will he reveal every detail of his plan. So, the next time you cannot see clearly, pray. Begin to give God the glory and trust in him to guide you through. He told me that the fog represents His Glory and he wants us to see just how much we need him. He wants us to recognize that he is present in and through it all. It is in the fog (glory) that we receive peace. It is in the fog (glory) that we learn to trust in Him more. It is in the fog (glory) that we receive instructions. Let go and allow Him to usher you into his presence. He will show you just enough to take the next step. Do not fear the unknown, release and walk into My Glory says the Lord...

Exodus 24:12-18

What If God?

I was thinking about how God knows what we will do prior to us doing it and I wondered why he allows it. Then this thought came to me; what if God allows it so we can be reminded of who He is? What if He allows it for us to stay on the path of righteousness? What if He knocks us down to humble us because he knows our troubles will ultimately lead us back to his love? Our trials tend to make us drop to our knees and cry out to God. We learn what not to do again and realize just how much we need Him. They show us who we really are without Him. Now, take a moment to praise Him for your trials and for the glory that will come after this!

Read Isaiah 55:8-9; 1 Corinthians 1:27-29

Don't Let Your Trials Trump Your Thanksgiving

Before I can open my eyes, the enemy is already at work trying to overload my mind with all that is going on in my life. I speak the truth when I say that it is not easy to be positive and have faith when you are experiencing challenges. The only way I found to be successful in overcoming them is to focus on God. I encourage you to speak His Word and praise him despite what you are going through. Take some deep breathes in then breath out and release your cares to Him. It all boils down to a choice. Will you choose to sink deep into your thoughts and worry or will you trust that God will make a way?

Read Psalm 118:24; 1 Thessalonians 5:16-24

The Green Pasture

As I was reading and meditating on the Lord, I saw sheep of all sizes eating. They were grazing the fields, and there was no brown grass or dirt in sight. Then suddenly, these thoughts started to download in my mind:

1 - We are the sheep of God's pasture and he will never let us go hungry. It is only when we stop feeding off, 'The Green Pasture', that we suffer hunger. We become subject to negative thinking and will begin to crave and entertain the wrong people and things.

2 - God is life and everything about who he is and what he does gives life. The grass not being brown showed me that God provides all the nourishment we need. There is no drought or lack when it comes to Him. So, when we experience different challenges, our confidence must remain solid in Him. He will supply all our needs daily and will not withhold anything good from us.

3 - The sheep variations in size showed me that we are not all supposed to look alike and be the same. We do not all eat the same amount of food, so our faith is not on the same level as others and some people are a little feebler. Ultimately it is up to us to choose how much we will hunger and thirst after God. You can provide someone with what they need, but it is up to them to receive it.

Read Psalm 23:1-2, 34:8-10 and 95:7-8

Make Me Like The Tree Planted By The River

The Lord will sometimes use the simplest things to speak to us. I was reading the seventeenth chapter of the book of Jeremiah and I could not get pass the seventh and eighth verses. It talks about the state of a person who puts their trust in the Lord and how they are like trees whose roots are spread out by the river. This is the revelation that I received. The more we trust in the Lord, the least affected we will be when trouble comes. We get our substance to survive and thrive from Him. When our roots (our faith in Him) are deep and are spread out by the river (His means of providing for us), we will never lack. We will always be in a prosperous state despite our situation and are protected from the dry seasons because we are grounded in Him. In fact, we do not see it as such because we are so consumed by Him. Our substance comes from deep within, not from what we can see, nor by our own strength. I want you to think of yourself as this tree. Tell yourself that you are prosperous and will never lack. Thank the Lord and let him know how much you need him. Be like the tree planted by the river and draw your strength from Him.

Read Psalm 1:1-3 and 128:1-2; Isaiah 12; Jeremiah 17:7-8; John 4:14

Be Careful To Leave The Doors Closed

I dreamt that I was running away from a dangerous situation and I saw this door cracked open. Although I was moving in the right direction, my curiosity aroused causing me to go back and see what was there. There were three different ways to get into this same door, and it was gray and brown stuff blowing outside of it. Then, I saw what appeared to be demon faces at the entrances and I heard the Lord say, "Be careful to keep the doors closed and do not look back." This is the word I received to release.

1) As the wind was blowing my feet started to get cold and it was harder for me to move to shut it back. Do not be afraid to leave the people and things God is calling you away from. Leaving doors open will cause you to have cold feet when it is time to move. Walk away while you have the chance and the courage to do so. When you leave, do not allow yourself to wonder about what is going on in their lives because it is none of your business.

2) The Lord gives us signs of the danger ahead. It may come in the form of someone we know, a stranger or some other way that is relatable. Whatever method He uses, we must be receptive to it.

3) The enemy awaits your return to the door. The faces at the entrance of the door represented the strength of the evil one. Returning to a place you have been delivered from will be harder to resist, so you can never underestimate his power and influence. Although we as

believers have Holy Spirit in us, we still cannot play around with the enemy. Playing on his ground or level is never fair game, so walk away and leave the doors closed. You have been warned says the Lord.

Read Genesis 19:10-11, 26; Luke 9:57-62; James 4:7

It's Ruff But It's Worth It

As I lay before the Lord, I just began to thank Him for His grace. I thought about some of the things that I have done and how I did not deserve a pass for it, but God! I said to myself, what I am going through now, can never outweigh what God has and is doing for me. Lord, it is ruff, but it is worth it! His mercies are new every morning and his grace is enough regardless of what I face in life. Think about what Jesus went through for us. He walked on that long road to the hill, just to die for us. He took the beatings, ridicule, rejection denials and death, all for us. So, why can't we for Him? Set your mind on the greater gain of eternal life with Him. Set your mind on what He suffered just for you. Now ask yourself, is it worth it?

Read Lamentations 3:19-26; Matthew 27:27-31; 1 Peter 3:17-18

L.O.V.E.

Sometimes God must discipline us with a firm hand, and it hurts. We must learn to take it willingly and understand that it is because of love. Love will not leave you and love will not let you stay in a mess.

Love
Opens
Various
Emotions

So do not get caught up in your feelings when God corrects you, embrace it, take heed and change. His LOVE sets you free!

Read Hebrews 12:5-11

Lean On Him Not Them

Too often we find ourselves leaning on the wrong things and people to make it. You will never find full security in anything on this earth. No amount of money or power can outdo what God can for you. You must learn how to depend on the Lord to make it. Examine yourself and let go of the things you have been leaning onto. May God give you the strength to do so in Jesus name.

Read Deuteronomy 8:3; Psalm 118:8; Proverbs 3:5-6; John 15:4-5

Can't See For Looking

We see but are we really seeing? We get lost while looking too deep into things and we put too much emphasis on and waste time on things that are not at all what they appear to be. You may be looking at your current situation as bad, but can you see an end to it? Being overly observant can cause us to miss out on our deliverance and blessings. I have been guilty of this, but I thank God for revealing His truth to me. If we continue to focus on what we do not have, we will miss enjoying what he has already blessed us with. The enemy desires to keep us seeing by looking. We must learn to see by hearing and believing.

Read 2 Kings 6:15-17; Romans 10:17; 2 Corinthians 5:7

Move Us Then Use Us

Sometimes we can get in the way of what the Lord is wanting to do in our lives. Take a moment and look at what you are enduring and ask yourself am I in God's way? I have a saying that God gave me, "Put self on the shelf." We must learn how to get out the way and let God have his way.

Read Matthew 26:39; John 3:30

Safe

When I think of the word safe, the first thing that comes to my mind is an umpire at a baseball game. We are thrown pitches in life, and our goal is to knock the ball out the park. Sometimes we miss or may even strike out, however the outcome, you must stay in the game. As you travel from base to base, there are people in front and behind you, counting on you to run. God will put people in your life who you will follow, others will rely on you, and some will push you and hold you accountable. It is not about you and you are not in this by yourself. We are all part of one body, running to get to the home base, heaven. Once we get there just like the umpire yells, "Safe", God declares the same thing. We are safe and secure from ever experiencing the condemnation that is due to us. Not only is our eternal security locked, but day to day God is keeping us safe from the enemy.

Satisfied our debt
And made us
Free from
Eternal condemnation.

Read 2 Samuel 22:4; Psalm 91; Proverbs 18:10; 2 Thessalonians 3:3; 1 Peter 1:3-5

Unstoppable

We get a glimpse of the victory and get discouraged when calamity hits. In most battles there will be some casualties and things are lost. Likewise, in our spiritual battles, our flesh is crucified, and things are removed. Some things we face will not be easy and the process can be difficult to endure. Be encouraged and know that when God is for you, nothing will be able to stop the work he is doing in and through you. Do not get discouraged during the process of elimination. Get up, dust yourself off, keep pressing and shout, "With God I am unstoppable!"

Read Isaiah 54:17; Romans 8:31; Philippians 1:6

He Loves Me

No matter what you do or go through God loves you! He loves you through your good and bad times. His love can reach us in the lowest place of our lives and it never runs out. Open your heart and receive His love and forgiveness today. Make it personal and tell yourself, "God loves me!"

Read Romans 8:37-39

Unclog The Drain

Our drains in our home had been clogged up for a while, until one night my husband decided to try to get it unclogged. He was at it for a while and he grew frustrated to the point he threw up his hands and called on the Lord for help. After a few more minutes and a bit more effort, the water started to flow.

As we walk in life things happen that clog up our spiritual drains. This drain catches all the mess and filth that God cleanses us of. When this happens, we need to call on the Lord to unstop it and he will give us strength to do our parts. Will you allow the Lord to unstop your drain today?

Read Psalm 50:15, 51:1-10; Philippians 4:13

Riding With The Son

I was taking my daughter to work one morning, and the sun was so bright I could barely see. Then, this thought came to me "Riding with the Son." I was determined to get her to her destination, so I pressed despite my view. God allowed me to see just enough to keep going.

Your yes to the Lord did not come easy and the enemy does not stop messing with you just because you are saved. Following Jesus requires for us to deny ourselves daily. We must trust in His guiding light to get us through to the end. He will show us just enough for us to keep pressing on. It will get tuff, and we will have challenges in life, but we will make it.

Read Psalm 119:105; Matthew 16:24; John 8:12; 2 Corinthians 5:7

Let God Fill It

We must stop seeking for man to do what only God can do for us. I spent a lot of time looking for things to fill the empty places in my life. I tried men, money, material things, sex, partying, friendships and whatever else I thought would fill the void, but I still felt incomplete. Now, there is nothing wrong with having some of these things. It was when I tried to use them to fill a place that only God could fill that it was not good for me. As I began to let go and let Him fill these vacancies, my eyes opened more to the truth. Learn to love God and He will teach you how to love yourself. When we seek Him first, the pleasures that we desire in life will eventually come. We tend to get impatient and try to jump ahead of God, do not do that. Lose yourself in Him and you will find yourself. He will deliver you and fill every void in your life!

Read Deuteronomy 6:5; Psalm 37:4-7; Matthew 6:33, 10:39

God Provides

As I was watching my children play, my attention was drawn to the back of my house. I found a bird's nest that someone had knocked onto the ground. I just stood amazed at how God provides for everything that he created. If God blessed the birds with a nest to live in, how much more will he do for us?

God will make a way somehow, so relax your mind and let your soul be at ease. Take time to look at the little things. Look at the flowers and how they bloom so effortlessly. Look at the birds and how they peck in just the right place to get the worm. No matter what you endure, have faith and know that God will provide.

Read Matthew 6:26-34

God Covers Me

I sometimes reflect on the things I have done since I have been saved and it is a wonder that I am still here. Sometimes we can be so hard on ourselves after making a mistake. If we have truly surrendered to the Lord and accepted Him, then the blood that was shed covers us. Now, I am not saying use it as an excuse to live sinful lifestyles. God looks at our hearts and He knows our true intentions.

I thank God that he does not write me off when I fall short of his Word. I believe that when He sees me, he sees purpose, he sees mercy, he sees the blood of his Son covering me. So, when you fall short remember God is covering you. Stop allowing yourself to get worked up because you fell. Get up, regain your footing and keep it moving, each day is another day to do better.

Read Psalm 51; John 10:27-30; Romans 3:23 , 6:1-6, 7:21-25; 1 Thessalonians 5:22-24

Reset And Reload Your Mind

Back in the day our gaming systems had game cartridges. When the game messed up we pushed the button to restart it and if that did not work, we would take it out, blow in it and put it back in.

Reset- Whatever you are worried about, shut down your thoughts and start over.

Reload- Speak the Word over that situation (blow in it) breath=life and the Word is life to us. Then, get back in there and keep yourself armed with Word.

Read Proverbs 4:20-22, 18:21; 2 Corinthians 10:3-5; Hebrews 4:12

Be Grateful

I was talking to someone and they were sharing with me the things that they had been going through. They told me about their health issues, living conditions and how much things were wearing them down mentally. I was thinking, now this cannot be true, but it was. It was so bad I wondered how they are still alive and able to handle it. You see, we complain and worry about stuff and do not realize there is someone who will gladly trade places with us. Take the time to reflect on your life, living arrangements and what God has done for you. What you have and where you are really is not as bad as you think, especially when you look around and see there is someone worse off than you. Humble yourself and be grateful; even in your struggle you are blessed.

Read Job 1:20-22; Psalm 106:1; Philippians 4:11-12; 1 Thessalonians 5:18

Adjust Your Focus

When I was younger, we had this little black and white television and on occasion, we would get a fuzzy picture. When that happened, we were told to either turn the knob a bit, change the channel or stick a hanger where the antenna was supposed to be. After messing with it for a while, it would clear up. This is where I am going with this.

1- Look to God. When we experience cloudy days and cannot see clearly, we need to go back to the basics. What did your spiritual leaders teach you about God?

2- Do not give up. We must use what we have learned about Him and keep using it until we see results; try and try again.

3- Change your mindset. The antenna represents our minds. Sometimes we get so messed up from all the stuff we have been through and our minds need to be fixed. Do not neglect your mind, make sure to renew your mind daily. Read the Bible, live it and trust God for everything.

Read Matthew 7:7; Luke 18:1-5; Romans 12:2; Hebrews 12:2; James 1:22

Don't Worry, Live And Be Happy

Too often we get caught up in our feelings and worry about things that are beyond our control. The Bible tells us not to worry and to give all our cares to the Lord. It is a process, but we must learn to transfer our burdens in exchange for God's peace. You cannot operate in faith if you continue to live in your feelings. Stop worrying about the things you cannot change and have absolutely no control over. Give them to God and let him handle it. Let go of the past, live for today and do not bother looking into the future. It will all come together in due time and your worrying about it will not make it happen any faster. Be free of worry today in Jesus name!

Read Matthew 6:25-34, 11:28-30; Philippians 4:6-7; 1 Peter 5:6-7

Cry It Out

I want to talk about two types of tears, tears of pity and tears of release. Tears of pity lead to depression, anxiety, bondage and frustration. Tears of release lead to deliverance, freedom, peace and comfort. To be honest, I do not like to cry. When I cry tears of pity, I find myself in such a lonely and empty place, bound by my fears. When I cry tears of release, I am at my weakest point and I can feel the peace of God more. It literally feels like God is wrapping me in his arms.

Our tears represent our silent cries to God, so do not stop them from falling. When we cry, He steps in because our tears are saying, Lord I need you, I cannot do this by myself. These are the words that He has been waiting to hear. So, cry until you feel that peace and comfort from God. Be encouraged in the Lord.

Read Genesis 21:16-17; Psalm 34:17-18, 56:8-9, 126:5; John 11:35

Look Again

We will never face anything in life alone, in all we endure God is with us and it will eventually work out for our good. It may not feel like it, but God is for you and because he is, nothing will be able to stand against you and win. I challenge you to begin to speak that against every negative report, person, and situation in your life. No matter what it is never doubt that God can do it. Even if the issue itself does not change, your attitude about it should. So, look again and this time see it through eyes of faith. Be encouraged in the Lord!

Read Isaiah 54:17; Daniel 3:14-18; Luke 1:37; Romans 8:28-31; 2 Corinthians 5:7

I Feel Like Going On

Every now and then we hit what I like to call, "Funk Bumps." These roadblocks, tests, trials and moody days only come to make us stronger. These experiences reminds us of 3 things;

1. Where we come from
2. We have not arrived and
3. God's grace is more than enough to get us through.

Refuse to look at your situation as a setback rather see your funk bump as an opportunity to grow. Speak over yourself and say, "No matter what I am going through, I can take it, I will make it and I feel like going on!" God did not bring you this far to leave you.

Read Jeremiah 29:11; 2 Corinthians 12:9

War Wounds

Battle scars from being on the battlefield, you have scars on your heart, mind and some on your body. They all serve as a reminder of where God has brought you from. Do not get lost in the battle and wave your white flag. Every scar from hurt, disappointment, failure and whatever else that has left an impression on you, was left for you to see that God is able. There is nothing too hard for Him!

You may be beat down, busted up and disgusted, but thank God you are still here. Look at your scars with joy and say, "If He did it before, He will do it again!"

Read Genesis 17:9-13, 32:24-32; Judges 16:28

Your Situation Is A Set Up For God To Shine

In the Bible, there was a man who was sick for thirty-eight years. There was a pool that the sick would lay by and at a certain time, the waters would be troubled and the first one in would be healed. Jesus came on the scene and asked the man if he wanted to be healed. The man replied that he did not have anyone to put him in the water and that other people beat him to it. Then Jesus told the man to get up, take up his bed and walk.

Stop relying on others to get you to your deliverance. Get desperate for the Lord and seek him yourself for what you need. You do not have to wait on your next check or appointment, all you need is an encounter with Jesus. It does not matter how long you have been down, be encouraged and know that your situation is just a set up for God to shine!

Read Psalm 42:1; John 5:1-16, 11:4

Dressed Up Mess

It is time for us to be real with ourselves and admit we need change. Sometimes our bad experiences break us to where we just cover them up. Over time, this accumulates damage we fail to realize is taking place. We must stop masking our hurt and deal with it because we only fool ourselves by faking. Remove the mask and be whole today in Jesus name.

Read Psalm 51; James 1:22-24

Think Before You Speak

Our words frame our attitude and actions. They can also determine how people perceive us and how they respond to us. We do not need to speak everything that comes to our minds. Be careful to make sure that your words are spoken in love and are guided by the Lord.

Read Proverbs 15:1-2; James 1:19, 3:5-10

God Sees The Best In Me

The Apostle Paul stated that he was the worst of sinners, but God used him to preach the gospel and he wrote a good portion of the New Testament. Stop making excuses and quit saying you are not good enough for God to use you. If God raised up Paul who persecuted and killed Christians, then surely, he can use you. Repent, surrender and let God use you! Your life may be what He uses to show others just how merciful he really is.

Read 1 Timothy 1:12-17

What Are You Afraid Of?

We tend to stay away from the things that we fear. We fear stepping out because of not knowing where we are going and what lies ahead. We fear promotion because of responsibility. We fear loving again because our hearts have been broken so many times. Our past sometimes shapes us into someone God has not called for us to be. Fear is paralyzing and keeps us in bondage, but God has called for us to be free from it. Whatever your hidden fear is, allow God in to help you to get over and through it.

Read Psalm 27:1; Isaiah 41:10; 2 Timothy 1:7

Signed, Sealed, Delivered

In the natural realm we get warranties when we buy a new product. In the same sense, when we receive Christ, we become a new creation and we get a warranty/guarantee that never expires and cannot be broken. The Lord is the only one who can seal our fate. When we are connected to Him, we are sealed forever. Do not allow your faith to fail, establish yourself in the Word of God.

I speak to the dry places and I command water to spring forth. May you flourish today and may your hope in God be rekindled in Jesus name!

Read 2 Corinthians 5:5; Ephesians 4:30; Philippians 1:6

Exposed

The saying goes everything that goes on in the dark will come to light. Pray and ask God to shine light on the dark areas of your life. Then, when they are revealed repent of it and let God fill the vacancy. Be humble enough to recognize your flaws and need for change. No one is perfect and none of us have arrived.

Read Ecclesiastes 7:20; Matthew 12:43-45; Romans 3:23; Philippians 3:12; 1 John 1:8-10

Examine Yourself

Sometimes we can focus so much on other people's flaws, to where we fail to recognize our own short comings. Take time to put the spotlight on yourself and ask God to examine your heart, then you will see how imperfect you really are. From the President to the Pastor all the way down to little babies, we are all imperfect people. I think that once we realize our need for change, the better we will treat others. My prayer is that God will give us more patience to deal with others and ourselves.

Read Psalm 139:23-24; Lamentations 3:40; Matthew 7:1-5; 2 Corinthians 10:6; 1 John 1:8

From The Gutter To Grace

Too often we look at the condition of a man and count them unworthy for the task. Now, I am not saying we should not be wise and not use discernment, rather we must be careful that we are not being self-righteous in our ways. We should never get so high up to where we look down on others and not even consider extending a hand. Let us not forget where we came from; if God brought us out then he can bring them out. Show a little more love and long suffering to someone who is not like you. You never know, you may just be the voice of reason they heed to.

Read Acts 9:1-22; 1 Timothy 1:12-16

Make Room For Jesus

Do you have people that has come around your family for so long that everyone thinks they are related? Or you feel like since the person teaching you about Christ is saved then you are to? Just because you are connected to someone who is a believer does not mean you are saved nor does going to church. At some point in your life you will need to make a conscious choice from the heart to surrender, receive and serve the Lord. He does not barge in and take over our lives, we need to invite him in. Moving is not easy so when you open and let Jesus in, some things must go, and it might hurt to let go of them. Stop saying you will do it when you get it together because we cannot do anything without him. Will you make room for Jesus today?

Read Romans 10:9-10; Revelation 3:20

Faith That Moves Mountains

Some things will come by prayer and some by prayer and fasting, but all things come by faith. God hears our prayers and he moves when he sees faith. You see, all it takes is a little genuine faith to get God's attention. For this reason, I believe is why He said come to him as a child because children believe everything that you tell them and they are more innocent. Be like a child in faith today. Believe everything you read or hear preached from the Word of God that is by the Spirit of God. Get your faith up, believe and do not doubt! Speak the Word over every situation and watch God change things.

Read Isaiah 55:10-11; Matthew 17:20-21 ;Romans 10:17; James 1:6-8

Have A Seat

Some of us wonder how long the Lord will allow people to get away with things. God allows the good and the bad for a reason and reasons we will never fully be able to comprehend. We must take Him at his word that what he said he will bring it to pass. It may get hard at times but no matter what it looks like we must view it through our faith scope. God gave me this acronym for the word pew which is a bench we sit on.

Position yourself to hear
Expect God to answer
Wait on Him to do it.

So, stop worrying, take your seat, be patient and watch God work!

Read Proverbs 15:3, 16:4

1...2....3...PUSH

When a woman gets pregnant, she is supposed to go through 3 stages of pregnancy. I look at our spiritual life in the same sense. With each stage we will experience different feelings, highs, lows and the in between. But our joy through the process is that something beautiful is forming on the inside of us. When it is time to deliver, the pain intensifies and we need to get out what is in us or one, our baby dies or two we both die.

God has been forming something beautiful inside of you to bring forth. The pain you are experiencing now is because you are close to seeing the manifestation of it. It is time to push it out so that the Lord can use you.

Read Micah 4:9-10; John 16:21; Romans 8:18-22; James 1:4

Antsy Pants

I tell the truth when I say that I am often trying to figure out how things are going to work out. My mind is constantly going and sometimes faster than my feet can follow. I go to sleep wondering how things are going to come together and I wake up to the same. This only wears me down and leads to two things, stress and doubt. God does not want us to be this way. He wants us to have peace of mind and to truly believe that He will. So, whatever has you constantly on the run, turn it over to the Lord and let him give you rest from it.

Read Psalm 4:8; Mark 9:23; Luke 1:37; Philippians 4:6-9; Hebrews 11:6

Show Me A Sign

Often times we want God to show us a sign in order to believe and move forward. While there is nothing wrong with that, we must be careful because our asking could be doubt in disguise. The enemy will sometimes use that method of questioning to hinder the process. Sometimes God will give us a sign and sometimes not. Either way, we must learn to trust Him when we cannot see and move when we do not feel.

Read Genesis 12:1-5; Psalm 37:23; John 4:48, 20:24-29

I Was Made For This

The Lord will never assign anything to you that he has not prepared you for. While often we feel like it is the total opposite, it is not. I see it like this, we are working with a trainer who is pushing us to the max and every time they do, we resist the pressure to continue. When this happens, the trainer is steady pushing us and encouraging us to keep going. In like manner, Jesus knows how much spiritual muscle we have, so while it may feel like we are maxing out we really are not. When the Lord gives us a task, the load may get heavy but we will not break in the process of carrying it.

Read Matthew 11:29-30; John 21:6-11; 1 Corinthians 10:13; Philippians 4:13

Working Together Works

My youngest son was trying to ride his power wheel but was having a hard time trying to get it to go. His brother noticed him struggling and instead of picking a fight, he hopped on the back and said come on and preceded to take charge and ride with him.

We are all part of Gods family and will have disagreements with one another. We must learn to lift one another instead fighting and tearing each other down. Remember that we are one body and when one hurts, we all hurt.

Read Psalm 133:1; Galatians 3:26-28, 6:1-2

My Place Of Safety

Our chances of being hurt increases when we decide to do things opposite of God's will. Being saved does not make us exempt from troubles, if anything the enemy kicks it up a notch because he has lost us. This new life in Christ changes our perception of our issues because we know that despite what comes our way God is with us and he will see us through. Be encouraged under fire; afterwards you will come out as pure gold, shining brighter than before.

Read Psalm 27; 1Peter 1:6-7

Down But Not Out

Issues of life tend to weigh us down and the decisions we make can cause us to take cover and run away from God. If you are there now, be encouraged in the fact that it is not over, and God can still use you. We may be shaken; we may stumble and even fall but we cannot be moved. You are victorious so get up, there is still some fight left in you!

Read 2 Corinthians 4:8-10,16,17

Don't Put Your Trust In The Method

For many years I have stocked up on things, even overstocked. To the point where some called me a hoarder, however, I did not see it as such. I felt that if I had more than enough, then the security of my family would not crumble. It made me feel like I had control of things in my life. I did not want to get low and when I did, anxiety would set up in me. After reading Luke 12:24, it made me realize that I do not need to stockpile anything. You see, I had unconsciously been putting my trust in the method and not the Man. The Lord wants us to put our complete trust in Him. Although it is a process, we must learn to take it day by day. We must stop going bankrupt trying to store up. Let your method fall to the back, and trust in the Lord to supply your daily needs.

Read Luke 12:24

Flaws And All

If a human being can love us for who we are, why is it so hard to believe that God does too? In my opinion Gods love, and forgiveness is the hardest to receive. The more I think about it I cannot help but ask myself, why? Why can we not believe that He loves us? Why is it so hard to believe that he forgives us when we fall? How is it that we find it easier to restore relationships with people, but harder with God? He is the epitome of love and forgiveness. He is the one who created us. He is the one who enables us to love and forgive. Open your heart to Him and receive his love because he loves you flaws and all.

Faith to believe and
Live believing and
Accepting my finished
Work on the cross that redeemed you from
Sin. Jesus loves you, flaws and all

Read Romans 5:8

Grief

There were times that I knew the death of someone close to me was coming. There were also times that I was caught by surprise by someone dying. What I found was that it did not matter whether I knew or not. They both brought the same level of pain, deep seated hurt and emptiness inside. The permanent separation from someone you love is never an easy thing to cope with. I do not think anyone could ever prepare enough for the blow that death brings. We go through mourning in many ways. Some shut down and does not talk about it, some lose their minds, and some even their faith in God, just to name a few. There are two acronyms that I heard about the word, grief. One speaks on how some of us feel and the other is what God does.

Grasping the
Reality of someone we love, leave us for
   good
In our minds wishing we had just one more
    moment to spend with them, but are left
    to only
Embrace the memories we have of them,
    leaving us
Feeling upset, hurt, empty, lost and questioning why...

God
Relieving an
Individual of the suffering they may be
Enduring
Freeing them to be with Him forever

We will never fully know why people are called from this life when they are. But one thing I do know, God is with us. He will help us get through day to day, moment to moment. It is not easy, but the Lord makes it bearable for us, if we trust in Him to do so. In my moments of mourning, I choose to remember the good things and hold them close to my heart. I thank God for the time that he blessed me to have with them. When I do this, I experience His joy and peace and I can push through just a little bit better.

Father I pray for all who are experiencing mourning on today. Give them strength to endure, peace and comfort in the name of Jesus. Bless them to hold onto the memories you have allowed for them to gain. Keep their minds in your perfect peace. Fill the void that has been left and heal the hurt they feel. Lord with you they can make it. Please embrace them and give them all they need to get through. In Jesus name amen.

Read John 11:33-35; Hebrews 4:15

God Is Enough

Why is it when God gives us instructions, we must know every detail there is to know? Why is it so hard to just go forward and trust in Him to do what he said? I believe these questions derive from our human nature. We are incapable of fully understanding God, and why he wants us to do certain things. We are used to being in control and having some level of understanding. The struggle between the spirit and flesh can get intense at times. However, we must have faith so that when God tells us to do something, we can rest assured that He will be there for us. He has already mapped out the road for us to travel and given us all we need to be successful. We cannot rely on people to get us there, God will use them, but they are not our true source. God is enough for us in everything we go through in life.

Read Exodus 33:12-17

Help Lift Them Up

Why is it so hard to help and sincerely support another person's vision? Why is it easier to hate on them and strive against them? When you hinder someone else's work, it can slow the progress with your vision. God wants us to be helpful and to work together as one. In the Bible, when Daniel was promoted, he brought Shadrach, Meshach and Abednego up with him. So, let us do our best to model that example. When you glow up, light up someone else's world by pulling them up with you.

Read Exodus 17:9-12; Proverbs 3:27; Daniel 2:46-49; Romans 15:1-2; Philippians 2:4; Hebrews 6:10

Cast It All On The Lord

It is easier to hold on to the weight of the things that concern us. Most of us need to know how it is going to work out and knowing makes us feel as if we have control of the situation. The truth is we are not controlling anything. We may think it is going to work out one way then God will turn it in a different direction. Another issue we run into is that we tell our problems to the wrong people. God will put people in our lives that we can confide in and give us wise counsel but never to the degree we trust them more than we do him. We must learn to stop stressing over our cares and give them all to the Lord.

Read Psalm 55:22; Proverbs 3:5-6; 1 Peter 5:6-7

Give Praise, Be Patient And Stay In Prayer

As we go through our journey in life, all sorts of challenges will meet us along the way. I believe that for us to get through them we should focus on doing these three things; give praise, be patient and stay in prayer. As we offer our praise to God it brings us to a place of peace and refuge from our problems. When we practice being patient, we learn how to be content in the Lord despite what is going on. When we pray, it gives us access to commune with God.

Praise Pulls Us Away From Focusing On Our Problems

Patience propels us into a place of contentment

Prayer presses out the doubt and gives us a renewed hope and a peaceful spirit.

Read Romans 12:12; 1 Thessalonians 5:16-18

Do Not Let Your Problems Overshadow The Promise

There were periods of time in the Bible that the people of God experienced affliction and suffering before entering the promise. If we read about the exodus of the children of Israel, we will see that they had to go through the valley before walking into the promise and unfortunately some of them missed it. Abrahams wife, Sarah, was barren for years and watched her handmaid give birth to his first child before she received the promise of their son Isaac. Naaman was a notable man who had leprosy and the prophet Elisha told him to go wash himself in the Jordan River seven times and he would be healed. Can you imagine what went through his mind after dipping in all those times not seeing results until the seventh time? All I am saying is do not allow what you are seeing and going through cloud your perception in the spirit. If God said it then it will come to pass. You have come too far to give up now, keep on believing and keep holding on!

Read Genesis 15:3-4, 16:1-4, 21:1-3; 2 Kings 5:1, 9-14; Hebrews 4:1

Come Out Of The Pit

God has promised us a way of escape from the temptation we face in life. Whether you have slipped in it or sunken deep into it, it is not too late for you. I am reminded of a time when I backslid and was so deep into it, I just accepted my fate. I felt unworthy of Gods forgiveness and felt like since I had fallen so deep what was the use of even trying again. If this is how you feel, I have good news, God loves you and can bring you out despite how deep you have fallen in! Be sensitive to the people around you because God will sometimes use them to help you out. Move with haste when He shows you the way out because you are in danger of dying if you linger. Come out and be free in Jesus name!

Read Psalm 34:17-19; Isaiah 59:1; 1 Corinthians 10:13

Public Failure

There have been some things that have happened that has caused me to question some of the decisions I have made. Consequently, feelings surfaced that should not be a part of my thought process. These feelings started in my mind and worked out into my actions. I was having a moment of pity and I heard the Lord say, "It was not a loss but a gain." He let me know that it was all a set up for him to work a miracle so he could get the glory. We say, "Lord use me", then we begin to question when trials find their way to our door. It is all part of the process. God makes you a public failure to show himself strong in your life. So, take the humiliation with a grateful heart and trust God. In due time you will see why, just be still and believe.

Read Judges 16:23-31

Do Not Cave Under The Pressures Of Life

Jesus's brothers were pressuring him to go somewhere and do some things he that knew was not right. He knew their hearts and what would happen, so he was not moved by their pleas and mocking.

Some of us are facing the pressure of deciding what to do. In our hearts we know what to do but we are still struggling to make the call. I encourage you to do as Jesus did, do not cave under pressure and stand for what you know is right. It will be difficult, but you will feel relief once your decision is made.

Read John 7:1-9

About The Author

Qiana Tucker was born, raised and currently resides in, Indianapolis, Indiana. She has been married to her husband, Corey Tucker Sr., for over ten years and they have a blended family with six children - three boys and three girls. She enjoys spending time with her family, taking walks, writing, volunteering and helping others who are in need.

Qiana accepted Jesus Christ as her Lord and Savior at the age of eighteen years old. Since then, she has completed numerous courses in biblical studies and in April 2014, she became a licensed minister. She has served in various capacities in the ministry; Assistant Youth Director, Teen Ministry Leader, Intercessory Prayer Team Leader, Usher, Pastor's Assistant, Outreach Ministry Coordinator and was on the Praise and Worship Team. In the early part of 2018, she founded *Sister 2 Sister Rebirth Ministry Inc.*, an organization that helps women of all ages establish and build a relationship with Christ and each other through healing of the whole person and self-esteem.

Denola Burton
DenolaBurton@EnhancedDNA1.com
www.EnhancedDNAPublishing.com